Literacy and Second Language

Published in this series:

Literacy and Second Language Oracy

ELAINE TARONE
MARTHA BIGELOW
and KIT HANSEN

OXFORD
UNIVERSITY PRESS

OXFORD
UNIVERSITY PRESS

Great Clarendon Street, Oxford OX2 6DP

Oxford University Press is a department of the University of Oxford.
It furthers the University's objective of excellence in research, scholarship,
and education by publishing worldwide in

Oxford New York

Auckland Cape Town Dar es Salaam Hong Kong Karachi
Kuala Lumpur Madrid Melbourne Mexico City Nairobi
New Delhi Shanghai Taipei Toronto

With offices in

Argentina Austria Brazil Chile Czech Republic France Greece
Guatemala Hungary Italy Japan Poland Portugal Singapore
South Korea Switzerland Thailand Turkey Ukraine Vietnam

OXFORD and OXFORD ENGLISH are registered trade marks of
Oxford University Press in the UK and in certain other countries

ISBN 978-0-19-442300-7

Printed in Spain by Unigraf S. L.

For our parents:
Ernest Tarone and Betty Tarone
Patricia Dennis and Albert Bigelow
Thomas Hansen and Bran Hansen

Brief Contents

Detailed Contents

Acknowledgments

Most importantly, we wish to recognize and thank the Somali teens and adults who agreed to participate in our study. Their time is precious and we are so grateful that they were willing to spend the time to talk to us and complete our many different tasks. We thank Ali Osman for helping us recruit participants, and the Children's Home Society and the Somali Education Center for allowing us to use their space to meet participants. Thanks to Eileen Watson for being the first to welcome us into Cedar Riverside neighborhood activities in 2001 and for her wise counsel about how to proceed with our research in respectful ways.

This research was supported by the resources of the University of Minnesota in a number of ways. Two University of Minnesota Graduate School Grants in Aid of Research supported our research, one awarded to Elaine Tarone in 2002 and another in 2003 to Martha Bigelow, who also won a single-semester leave to gather data and immerse herself in the community. In 2004 Elaine Tarone and Kit Hansen were given a College of Liberal Arts Graduate Research Partnership Program grant. All these grants funded Kimberly Johnson, Larry Davis, Mike Hinrichs, and Becky Uran Markman, who helped us with research, transcription, and data analysis. Nora Wildgen White is the artist who drew pictures we used to gather the data (see Figure 3.2). The University of Minnesota has also supported our travel to numerous conferences to present versions of the papers upon which this book is based.

We are deeply grateful to Jenefer Philp, whose original study simultaneously anchored and inspired us. We wish to acknowledge Bonnie Swierzbin and Bob delMas, who were co-authors with us on papers published with the data reported in this book. We benefited greatly from feedback on earlier drafts of segments of this book by Michael Graves, Abukar Ali, Anne Lazaraton, Jim Lantolf, Lourdes Ortega, Merrill Swain, Henry Widdowson, Jill Watson, and George Yule. Mike E. Anderson provided weekly encouragement on getting this project to completion. Finally, we would like to thank our editor, Cristina Whitecross, with whom it has been such a pleasure to work.

Abbreviations

ACT	Adaptive Control Theory
EI	elicited imitation
ESF	European Science Foundation
ESL	English as second language
IL	interlanguage
L1	first language
L2	second language
LARC	Language Acquisition Research Centre
LESLLA	Low-Educated Second Language and Literacy Acquisition
NLLSD	Native Language Literacy Screening Device
NNS	non-native speaker
NS	native speaker
SLA	second language acquisition
SPEAK	Speaking Proficiency English Assessment Kit
TLU	target-like use
ZISA	Zweitspracherwerb Italienischer und Spanischer Arbeiter
ZPD	Zone of Proximal Development

Introduction: Questioning assumptions in SLA research

A prominent goal of research on second-language acquisition (SLA) is to identify universal cognitive processes involved in acquiring 'second languages',[1] or L2s. Yet there has been very little SLA research to date on the cognitive processes of illiterate or low-literate adult L2 learners.[2] Almost all the adult learners studied in SLA research have been literate, in the sense that they have been able to decode printed or embodied text. Typically, they have even been college students, such as undergraduates in foreign-language programs, graduate students in intensive English programs, or international teaching assistants. These L2 learners have all been initiated into the social practice of print literacy, which is an essential skill that affords them access to, and power in, the academic world. It is a skill providing access to many of academia's other literacies as well, including media and digital literacies.

But can these literate L2 learners be assumed to be representative of *all* L2 learners? Can we base an SLA theory of universal cognitive processes on data drawn only from literate learners? What about L2 learners who do not participate in the social practice of print literacy at all? These learners are sometimes referred to as 'preliterate' (Robson 1982). Such learners clearly exist in large numbers throughout the world, but we know next to nothing about their processes of oral second language acquisition. Because illiterate and low print literate L2 learners rarely if ever set foot in the social world of academia in which SLA researchers operate, they have been left out of the SLA database. For example, at least since 1990, ours has been the only study published in the *TESOL Quarterly* that documents the SLA processes of post-critical period L2 learners with low print literacy levels (Bigelow, delMas, Hansen, and Tarone 2006). To leave these learners out of SLA research is both to deny their existence or relevance and to deny them any educational benefits that might accrue for pedagogy, from our improved understanding of the way they may learn L2s differently from literate learners.

This omission is also important for theory generalizability. Theories need to account for major accepted findings in the field if they are to be viable (Long 1990). Of course, if those accepted findings are drawn only from

Population Y, and not from Population Z, then, as far as we know, our theory applies only to Population Y. If we want to know whether our theories apply to Population Z, then we will need to test them with data and findings from Population Z. This is the situation we currently face in the field of SLA. Virtually all of our findings on SLA are drawn from Population Y: a group of highly literate learners. We have almost no findings on the SLA processes of members of Population Z: low-literate and illiterate adult learners.

This omission restricts the usefulness and practical applicability of the entire SLA research enterprise. Illiterate and low-literate adults learn second languages all the time. As early as 1970, Hill stated that it was common for unschooled and illiterate individuals in remote places of the world to learn second languages. In 1980 and thereafter, some learners moved from those remote places of the world and into US cities. Large numbers of illiterate Hmong immigrants to the USA had an urgent need to learn English as an L2. Yet, when ESL teachers have asked SLA scholars for research-based advice, the scholars have had little to say to them that pertained directly to the SLA of illiterate learners. There was no research on the SLA processes of illiterate adults.

The cost of disregarding social context in SLA theory-building

The omission of low-literate or illiterate L2 learners from the SLA database can be viewed as an outcome of a more general theoretical problem in SLA research—namely, a general neglect of the social dimension in the process of SLA. In modeling L2 learner competence as an (undefined) abstraction, neutral in terms of its variable realization in different modes of use, SLA researchers have taken the position that social context simply does not matter (cf. Long 1998). Tarone (2000b, 2007, forthcoming) points out that SLA researchers have allowed their investigation of such crucial constructs as L2 learners' 'abstract competence', L2 'input', 'output', and even 'context/ setting' to be restricted to the laboratory-like environment of the academic world, a world that is more conducive to psycholinguistic than sociolinguistic thinking. She argues that major adjustments are needed if these concepts are to make any sense in the socially embedded experiences of L2 speakers in their own worlds. And she cites studies showing that social factors in fact influence the cognitive processes of L2 learners. For example, according to Bondevik (1996), salesmen in a Minnesota electronics store did not provide corrective feedback in the way ESL teachers on the UCLA campus did in Long's study (1980); Bondevik's findings raise questions about Long's claim that corrective feedback behavior is 'universal' (cf. Tarone 2007, forthcoming).

A very serious outcome of SLA researchers' construction of SLA as an abstract cognitive process, universal and unaffected by social context, is that it has led to a general failure to study the process of SLA as it is routinely engaged in by a whole range of populations of L2 learners in a range of social contexts outside schools and academia. As a consequence, we know very little about the process of SLA of such learners as: completely illiterate but bi- or multilingual learners in newly industrialized countries; unschooled (but possibly functionally literate) L2 learners in newly industrialized countries; immigrant and refugee L2 learners in low-wage jobs in industrialized countries. Indeed, we even know little about the way SLA occurs in classrooms and communities closer to home, or in learners with different individual or cultural learning styles from our own. To take just one example: how did Kao Kalia Yang, as a young Hmong refugee, manage to acquire oral English L2 in St Paul, Minnesota classrooms when, by her own account, she said almost nothing in her classes for years and years? She was not the traditional ESL learner that our SLA theories assume. Yet, as a graduate of Carleton College and author of a well-written memoir (Yang 2008), she was clearly a successful learner of L2 reading and writing. We do not know how she achieved this. We need longitudinal SLA studies of non-traditional L2 learners embedded in a range of real social contexts. Current SLA theory that minimizes the importance of social context leads to major omissions and gaps in our database such as these; models of SLA that incorporate social context, such as Preston (2000, 2002) and Lantolf (2000a), will help us address such omissions and gaps.

In this book, we would argue that the inclusion of less-literate L2 learners will contribute to SLA theory-building. Perhaps most fundamentally, it will enable us to examine the impact that some of our own uncritically accepted cultural assumptions and presuppositions, founded in our own literacy, have on our perceptions as researchers. In enabling us to do these things, research with this unstudied population will broaden our view of the nature of SLA and of the human potential for language learning.

The impact of native language literacy on second language literacy

As pointed out at the beginning of this chapter, there has been virtually no research on the impact of literacy on L2 oral skills; however, a good deal of research has documented the impact of first language (L1) literacy on the development of L2 literacy. Cummins (1991) has taken the position that L1 literacy facilitates learners' acquisition of L2 literacy. Collier (1989), for example, reviewed the published literature on L2 learner performance on standardized tests believed to correlate highly with academic language proficiency. One of the two major factors correlating positively with learners' academic literacy in the L2 in all these settings was whether the learners were literate in their L1. Adolescent L2 learners who were not literate in their L1 took seven to ten years to learn age-appropriate L2 literacy-related context-reduced and cognitively demanding academic language skills; some never seemed to catch up with their native speaking peers. Those who did have L1 literacy skills took less time to acquire comparable literacy skills in their

	Native language	Second language
Oral skill	1. L1 Oracy	3. L2 Oracy
Literacy skill	2. L1 Literacy	4. L2 Literacy

Table 0.1. Relationships between L1/L2 oracy and L1/L2 literacy

L2.[3] According to this research, the length of time to full academic literacy increases with age of onset of initial literacy.

However, scholars have not examined the impact of L1 or L2 literacy on L2 oral skills. Even recent major research initiatives fail to examine this. The research questions typically investigated by SLA scholars deal with relationships between literacy and oracy, such as:

1 What is the relationship between L1 oral skills and L2 literacy?
2 What is the relationship between L2 oral skills and L2 literacy?
3 What is the relationship between L1 and L2 literacy?

Table 0.1 offers another way of understanding these relationships; the focus of most research is on relationships of various cells to Cell 4: L2 literacy.

However, what has been missing is any exploration of the impact of L1 or L2 literacy (Cells 2 and 4) on Cell 3—the cognitive processing of oral L2. Using this table, we can better conceptualize such interesting research efforts as those of Keiko Koda and her colleagues (Koda 1989, 2005; Wang, Koda, and Perfetti 2003); these researchers have documented the impact of Cell 2 on Cell 4: literate learners' knowledge of different types of L1 writing systems (alphabetical versus logographic) on their phonological or semantic cognitive processing of reading materials in L2. Koda and colleagues, while they have perhaps come closest in their work to that explored in this book, carefully documenting the impact of different L1 writing systems on L2 reading and writing, have not, to our knowledge, explored the impact of this knowledge on Cell 3: learners' L2 *oral* processing. This omission has been widespread.

Summary

SLA research has not included the study of the way illiterate and low-literate (literate in either L1 or L2) adults process or acquire oral second languages, even though alphabetic print literacy is a very important 'individual difference' in adult L2 learning. This omission, just one consequence of the relative neglect of social context in theory-building in the field of SLA research, has seriously limited the validity of SLA theory and its applicability and usefulness. In the first decade of the twenty-first century, some twenty-five years after the first wave of illiterate Hmong refugees came to the USA, and even after subsequent in-migrations of other low-literate groups (Somalis, Karen, and so on), SLA researchers still have few applicable findings on the SLA processes of illiterate and low-literate learners. For this reason, they have little information to offer ESL teachers looking for answers about the oral SLA processes taking place in their classrooms. Study of 'non-traditionally studied' L2 learners such as these will help researchers to examine the impact of their own literacy on their assumptions and perceptions as researchers. In enabling us to do these things, research with this unstudied population will broaden our view of the nature of SLA and of the human potential for language learning, and contribute to the improvement of curricular and instructional practices with this group of L2 learners.

In this volume, we offer what we believe to be the first set of research studies on the oral SLA processes of low-literate learners. We will begin by providing the background for those studies. In Chapter 1, we review a body of research in cognitive psychology and child language acquisition that documents the impact of alphabetic literacy on native language oracy.

Notes

1 We will follow standard practice in the field of SLA research in using the term 'second language' to refer to any and all languages acquired after the native language; such languages may in fact be second, third, or fourth languages.
2 An encouraging recent development has been the 'Low-Educated Second Language and Literacy Acquisition (LESLLA) publications: Van de Craats, Kurvers, and Young-Scholten (2006) and Faux (2007).
3 This research does not imply that illiterate adolescents or adults who enroll in high school or adult basic education classes will take 7–10 years to finish. This research suggests only that the process of developing literacy to the level of native-speaking peers may take much longer than if the individual were literate upon arrival.

I

Alphabetic print literacy and phonological awareness

What is oracy? This construct represents for us the individual's ability to use a set of oral language processing and production skills in communication. Oracy roughly parallels literacy as a construct.

What is literacy? Broad definitions of literacy go beyond the traditional notion of being able to read and write, and focus on the individual's ability to communicate in particular social settings, time, and through multimedia such as computers, video, or the Internet. 'New Literacy Studies' (Gee 1991; Street 2003) explore and document the nature of literacy as social practice, and the way in which one or another specific social literacy practice may become dominant while others may be marginalized in society at particular times and places.

In this book, we readily recognize this broader social and political context for our study of literacy, and we situate our discussion in this context. Functional and sociocultural studies of literacy are extremely important in establishing this context and showing how literacy skills of all kinds function within it. However, we are primarily interested not so much in how literacy skills function in the wider society, but rather in the skills themselves—the skills that are required to process the media of speech and writing, sounds, and spellings, in alphabetic print literacy. Alphabetic print literacy has clearly become a dominant social practice in much of the world, and a means for the marginalization of those who do not practice it. We will use the term 'print literacy' to refer to the focus of interest of this book, and define it as the ability to encode and decode oral language units with an alphabetic script.

Other scholars have documented the broad differences between written and spoken language, regardless of type of written script, and many have been interested in the possible cognitive consequences of functioning in each modality. One long line of scholarly discussion has focused on the relationship between written language and thought. For example, Goody and Watt (1968) and Havelock (1978) argued that literacy promotes abstract concepts, analytical reasoning, and logic. Vygotsky (1978) felt that the ability to use written language as a sign system could transform intellectual processes, and Luria (1976) provided mixed empirical evidence that this was true. However, a careful study by Scribner and Cole (1981) showed that it is the sociocultural context of schooling, rather than literacy alone, that improves the performance of adults on a range of reasoning tests focused on abstraction, categorization, semantic memory, and logic. They showed that someone who is alphabetically literate is *no* better at higher-level reasoning skills than someone who uses only oral language. (Schooling, on the other hand, does improve higher level reasoning skills.)

Facets of print literacy

Print literacy itself is a complex construct. Ravid and Tolchinsky (2002) state that the mastery of written language involves two aspects: mastery (1) of written language as discourse style (that is, the recognition that the language used in writing is basically different from the language used in speech, and further, that there are many varieties of written language); and (2) of written language as notational system (the recognition and ability to produce the representational system used in writing). Verhoeven (1994) also divides literate competence into components: grammatical, discourse, (de)coding, strategic, and sociolinguistic competence; his grammatical and decoding components align with Ravid and Tolchinsky's idea of written language as notational system, while his discourse, strategic, and sociolinguistic competence seem equivalent to Ravid and Tolchinsky's notion of literacy as discourse style. (The latter has also been the focus of Biber (1988), Biber and Hared (1991), and Biber, Reppen, and Conrad (2002).) Similarly, Wiley (2005) divides research on literacy into two major orientations: the 'autonomous' orientation, which focuses on the formal properties of encoding and decoding text, as well as the individual cognitive consequences of this, and the 'social practices' orientation, which views literacy not as an individual property, but as an activity deeply embedded in social relationships. Wiley includes as proponents of the first orientation, Goody (1987), and Olson and Torrance (1991), and as proponents of the second Heath (1983), Gee (1991, 2001), and Street (1995). While Wiley discusses these two orientations as somewhat antithetical, we follow Ravid and Tolchinsky (2002) in viewing them as more complementary, and relating to different components of literacy itself.

As stated at the outset, in our work we focus on only a part of the large construct of literacy: the part that Ravid and Tolchinsky (2002) refer to as 'notational system', and what Verhoeven (1994) describes as the two literacy components of '(de)coding' and 'grammatical competence'. These are rather specific cognitive skills. We are particularly interested in the relationship between mastery of notational system skills and some specific oral language-processing skills. We further target the abilities of adults who are not literate, and, ultimately, the oral skills those individuals bring to the process of SLA.

Types of script

To begin with, we must distinguish among the various scripts that must be (de) coded in print literacy. The visual symbols in different types of *script* may represent oral language units of different sizes. In an ideal *alphabetic* script, each grapheme, or visual print symbol, represents a phoneme, or minimal sound segment having linguistic meaning in the language. In English, for example, the grapheme T regularly corresponds to the phoneme /t/. The spelling system of English has evolved over time in such a way that there is not always a one-to-one correspondence of this type. Some English phonemes, such as /iy/, may be represented by a range of different graphemes or grapheme combinations (for example, EE in the word 'green', EA in the word 'peach', E in the word 'gene', and so on). However, the script for representing English is still alphabetic: while it is not always a one-to-one relationship, the function of graphemes or groups of graphemes is to represent the phonemes of English. Syllabic scripts, used in writing languages such as Japanese, use a visual symbol to represent larger phonological units: syllables, such as 'ga', a consonant–vowel combination. Similarly, in the 'unpointed' writing system used to represent Hebrew, the orthographic unit usually corresponds to a CV syllable rather than a single phoneme (Ben-Dror, Frost, and Bentin 1995). In logographic scripts, used in writing languages such as Chinese, each visual symbol represents a semantic unit, such as a morpheme or a word like 'house'.

Alphabetic literacy and phonological awareness in a native language

Given the paucity of L2 research on the relationship between literacy and oracy, we turn first to a consideration of the large body of research on literacy and oracy in a native language. In this chapter we focus on just one kind of relationship between alphabetic literacy and oracy: the relationship between literacy and 'phonological awareness' (awareness of linguistic units in oral input). A robust body of research and scholarship in several related disciplines has focused on this relationship as it exists for monolingual children and for adults. In research on child language development, it has long been acknowledged that young children are not aware of words as phonological entities until about the age of 6 or 7, the age at which they also become literate (see Piaget 1929; Vygotsky 1962, 1978; Berthoud-Papandropoulou 1978). Olson (2002) describes empirical findings that support the view that children who cannot read believe that words represent entities themselves, and not linguistic abstractions. His team has conducted studies showing that, before they learn to read, children assume that written signs represent events and meanings rather than words or sentences about those events. For example, a child not yet able to read, who is asked to write 'cat', writes one scribble; when asked to write 'two cats', he writes two scribbles; 'three cats' is three scribbles. 'No cats' is a wave of the pencil in the air and a statement such as: 'There's no cats so I didn't write any-thing.' In another study, the child is shown a card that says 'three little pigs' and someone reads that phrase. Then one word is covered up and the child is asked to guess what it says now. The child says 'two little pigs', a response that reveals an assumption that the text relates to objects and events, rather than language *about* objects and events. Based on these responses, Olson concludes that the child who does not yet know how to read does not have the concept of 'word'. Thus, for Olson, it is literacy that leads to linguistic awareness.

Researchers on child literacy development agree that there is a strong relationship between literacy and phonological awareness (e.g. Durgunoğlu and Öney 2002). But there has apparently not been a consensus as to the *directionality* of this relationship. Does literacy produce children's linguistic awareness, as Olson claims? Or does the increasing linguistic awareness of the cognitively maturing child provide the foundation upon which literacy may be developed? This is a kind of chicken and egg problem.

In fact, it appears that Olson is in the minority; the majority of researchers on child language development and child reading development assume that phonological awareness comes first and is a prerequisite to learning to read. For example, Verhoeven (2002) cites Snowling (1998: 487):

> readers activate speech codes during the decoding process—even in
> morphemic writing systems such as the Chinese. As such, literacy
> acquisition depends critically upon a child's speech processing skills.

Reading researchers such as Thompkins and Binder (2003) also assume that prior phonological awareness results in higher reading scores. Noting that it is well known that phonological awareness and reading level correlate strongly in studies of children, they propose to examine the same relationship among adults who are functionally illiterate, and compare the results to those of children. They compare the phonological awareness and short-term memory skills of 60 functionally illiterate adults matched with a group of 99 children of similar reading abilities, finding that the adults rely less on phonological decoding and more on remembering specific words and patterns, and general world knowledge or experience. They frame the results of the study in terms of identifying which phonological and memory skills account for (i.e. cause) the greatest amount of variance in reading level scores.

However, as we have noted, there are some in child language develop-ment who have taken the opposite position: that it is the development of the decoding skill that causes increased phonological awareness. Berthoud-Papandropoulou (1978) has stated that the development of children's awareness of words as phonological forms depends on their exposure to written words. Indeed, many of the scholars described by Wiley (2005) as having an 'autonomous' orientation[1] to the study of literacy (e.g. Olson 2002) have argued quite strongly that it is the process of becoming literate that provides individuals with an awareness of the linguistic units encoded in the notational system of the written language, which in turn can increase awareness of those linguistic units in the oral modes. So, in discussing the impact of literacy on children's cognition, Olson (2002: 158) has put it this way: 'Children's important discovery is that their own and others' more or less continuous speech may be thought of as a sequence of lexical items or "words".' Indeed, Olson (1994) argues that alphabetic literacy not only raises awareness of the phonemic and lexical structure of language. He argues that the units of analysis of oral language that are used in linguistics derive from alphabetic systems of writing. 'Awareness of linguistic structure is a product of a writing system…' (Olson 1994: 68).

But it is difficult to establish directionality between phonological awareness and literacy development when working only with a population of children, where age, cognitive development, and literacy level are typically confounded. Perhaps the directionality of this relationship is best explored in carefully designed studies of adults who are illiterate, because literacy level can be easily separated from age and cognitive development.[2]

Oral language processing and adult illiteracy

As established in our Introduction, there are a great many illiterate adults throughout the world, so it is quite feasible to study highly comparable groups of adults whose only distinction is their ability to encode and decode written language. If groups of literate and illiterate adults who share all other characteristics (for example, intelligence, culture, gender, age) differ in their performance of oral language awareness and manipulation tasks, then it seems much more likely that the causal factor is the single variable that distinguishes those groups: literacy.

Ong has written eloquently about his views on the impact of literacy on human cognition. Describing the characteristics of 'oral cultures' versus 'literate cultures', Ong maintains that the organization of pre-literate expression is basically formulaic, with substantial use of proverbs and other set expressions. It is 'additive' rather than 'subordinating and analytic'; redundant, not efficient; interactive, not objective; situational, not abstract (Ong 1982). Literacy changes this, Ong argues, bringing about a shift to parsimony, analysis, distance, and abstraction—nothing less than a transformation of human consciousness. Ong provides minimal research evidence to support this vision. Indeed, Lantolf points out that the distinction between oral and written language is not as categorical as Ong suggests, because the oral language of even very literate speakers is full of formulae and fixed expressions (personal communication, July 15, 2008).

More recent research on the oral processing abilities of adult illiterates has been carried out in Brazil and Portugal by a team of researchers in the field of cognitive psychology and neuropsychology (e.g. Morais et al. 1979; Morais et al. 1986). These studies set up experimental and control groups of adults living in the same social groups who shared a wide range of social and intellectual variables, but differed only in that one group could decode alphabetic script and the other group could not. The results of these studies suggest that the acquisition of the ability to decode an alphabetic script changes the way in which the individual processes oral language.

The original goal of these researchers (publishing in such journals as *Cognition*, *Cognitive Neuropsychology*, and *Applied Psycholinguistics*) was to document the incidence of cognitive impairments of various kinds within a larger population of adults in Brazil and Portugal, many of whom were also illiterate. In order accurately to separate cognitive impairment from normal illiterate functioning, they needed to establish a baseline of oral language performance by normally functioning illiterate adults. Morais, Cary, Alegría, and Bertelson (1979), and Morais, Bertelson, Cary, and Alegría (1986) found that, while many illiterate adults in their studies performed oral tasks focusing on rhyme or on the analysis of speech into syllables just as well as literate adults did, they performed far worse on oral tasks requiring segmental analysis or manipulation, particularly at the level of the phoneme. These researchers have argued that an individual's mastery of an alphabetic script, which requires a grapheme–phoneme correspondence, establishes the ability of literate adults to process oral language in terms of the linguistic segment 'phoneme'. A corollary to that argument is that illiterate adults with minimal awareness of the linguistic construct 'phoneme' have difficulty performing oral phonological tasks that require that awareness.

Oral linguistic awareness tasks in these studies could focus on linguistic units at several levels: the phoneme, the syllable, or the word. Generally these kinds of tasks were relatively easy for literate adults and almost impossible for illiterate adults; Adrian, Alegría, and Morais (1995) provide the following examples of tasks differentiating literate and illiterate adults in Spain.

Phoneme deletion and reversal tasks:

- 'If we subtract [t] from the syllable [tal], we have…?' 'Answer: [al].'
- 'How would you say [los] backwards?' 'Answer: [sol].'

Syllable deletion and reversal tasks:

- 'If we subtract [de] from the word [kade], we have…?' 'Answer: [ka].'
- 'Say [taro] backwards.' 'Answer: [rota].'

Word reversal task:

- 'Say zanahoria rota backwards.' 'Answer: rota zanahoria.'

In contrast, Adrian and colleagues showed that tasks like the following showed no difference in the performance of literate and illiterate adults:

- Phonetic discrimination (e.g. 'ta-sa': same or different?).
- Rhyme detection (e.g. 'mepu/pepu': rhyme or not?).
- Syllable detection (e.g. is [pa] contained in [pati]?.
- Phoneme detection (e.g. do these words contain the same phoneme? [kar kus]).

Other tasks that have shown significant differences between literate and illiterate adults include 'phonological fluency' tasks, where they are given one minute to list all the words they can think of that start with a named phoneme (e.g. /t/). But 'semantic fluency' tasks, where they have one minute to list all the members of a semantic class (e.g. animals, plants), are not difficult at all, producing no differences between literate and illiterate adults. Kolinsky, Cary, and Morais (1987) used a word-awareness task, and found that awareness of phonological length of words was also related to literacy. Finally, word and pseudoword repetition tasks have shown literacy differences. Literate and illiterate adults are equally good at repeating known words like 'banana', but illiterate adults are significantly worse at repeating pseudowords (created by replacing consonants of a known word) like 'gamama'.

What is the influence of a non-alphabetic as opposed to an alphabetic script? Read, Zhang, Nie, and Ding (1986) focus on two comparable groups of adult Chinese participants, both educated and both living in a similar context of social practice. One group (*n* = 18) was literate only in Chinese characters, having been educated in schools that had not yet adopted the Chinese alphabetic script (Hanyu Pinyin). The second group (*n* = 12), comparable to the first in level of education, age, and social group, had become literate in both Chinese characters and the alphabetic script. Their differential exposure to an alphabetic script was an accident of history and social change, and was not due to any differences in their cognitive ability or their social situation. Both groups were asked to perform oral tasks in Chinese; they were asked to add or delete a single consonant (*d, s, n*) at the beginning of a spoken syllable. All syllables and targets were possible words in Chinese (e.g. /an/, /san/); some targets were words and some were non-words. The results showed that in this task the adults who had alphabetic literacy significantly outperformed those who did not. Where the targets were non-words, the alphabetically literate adults' accuracy was 93 percent compared to 37 percent for the group that was not alphabetically literate; for targets that were words, the adults with alphabetic literacy achieved an 83 percent accuracy rate compared to 21 percent for the adults without it. The authors conclude that, for most adults, the ability to segment oral language develops *as a consequence* of the process of learning to read and write alphabetically. A similar study on Chinese readers by de Gelder, Vroomen, and Bertelson (1993) replicated Read and colleagues' results.

Similar studies were subsequently carried out in Spain, Portugal, and Brazil, to compare the performance of adults who were, or were not, literate. For example, Adrian, Alegría, and Morais (1995) administered an extensive battery of oral tasks to a group of fifteen illiterate adults in Spain, comparing their performance to that of two other groups: one a group of 'poor readers' and the other a group of 'readers'. The illiterate participants scored as well as the literate ones on a phonetic discrimination task asking participants whether pairs such as /me-me/ or /sa-ta/ were different. This showed that literacy did not affect phonological sensitivity. Half the illiterate participants did very well on rhyming tasks, so literacy had a negligible effect on this skill. However, the illiterate participants got very low scores on all tests that required conscious awareness of phonemes (matching, monitoring, deletion, and reversal). They were also significantly worse than the literate adults on oral tasks requiring them to reverse words and syllables.

Research on phonological awareness of illiterate adults

Reis and Castro-Caldas (1997: 445) provide the clearest summary we have found of the theoretical implications of this body of research comparing the way illiterate and literate adults perform phonological awareness tasks:

> Learning to match graphemes and phonemes is learning an operation in which units of auditory verbal information heard in temporal sequence are matched to units of visual verbal information, which is spatially arranged. This type of treatment of auditory verbal information modulates a strategy in which a visual–graphic meaning is given to units that are smaller than words, and thus independent of their semantic representation. Children need to be aware of phonology in order to segment the continuum of the oral language. After being isolated as significant units, these segments are introduced sequentially in a working memory system (Baddeley 1995) that is present from the early stages of language acquisition, and to which a new content of visual experience is added. If we, as normal adult readers, are asked to spell a word, we evoke a visual image of its written form. The awareness of phonology also allows us to play with written symbols (which can be transcoded to sounds) to form pseudoplausible words, independently of semantics. Therefore, learning to read and write introduces into the system qualitatively new strategies for dealing with oral language; that is, conscious phonological processing, visual formal lexical representation, and all the associations that these strategies allow.

To explore this general postulate, Reis and Castro-Caldas (1997) studied two groups of women in a fishing community in the south of Portugal, matched for intelligence and family/cultural environment and differing solely in terms of their knowledge of the phonemic value of a set of graphemes. Indeed, the matched pairs of subjects were sisters in families where the eldest sister had always been required to stay home from school to take care of her younger siblings and had never learned to read, while her younger sisters had been allowed to go to school and learn to read. In this traditional culture, the sisters had returned to live out their lives in the same fishing village as wives and mothers, with minimal to no role for literacy in their lives. They were now much older, in their fifties and sixties, and their oral language processing in Portuguese was tested by Reis and Castro-Caldas, who administered a set of simple oral language tasks.

Postulating that the illiterate sisters would rely primarily on semantic strategies rather than phonological strategies to perform certain oral tasks, the researchers conducted three experiments: (*a*) an oral word versus pseudoword repetition task; (*b*) an oral word-pair memory task, where some pairs were semantically related and some were phonologically related; and (*c*) verbal fluency tasks that were either semantic (e.g. names of plants) or phonological (e.g. words that begin with /t/). In Experiment (*a*), the illiterate group found repetition of pseudowords significantly more difficult than the literate group, while both groups did equally well on repetition of real words in frequent usage. In Experiments (*b*) and (*c*), the semantic word pairs were significantly easier for the illiterate group than the phonological ones, and the semantic verbal fluency task was significantly easier than the phonological one. Overall, the illiterate group did comparatively worse than the literate group on both semantic and phonological tasks in Experiments (*b*) and (*c*). The experimenters concluded that the illiterate participants relied primarily on strategies that were good for semantic processing but not for phonological analysis, while the literate participants could use both semantic and phonological strategies at once. This ability to use both kinds of strategies greatly improved the accuracy of the literate group. In their conclusion, Reis and Castro-Caldas (1997) suggest that semantic processing is implicit, while learning to read and write provides individuals with an explicit dimension in the process of phonological processing. Their fundamental conclusion is that illiterate adults' inability to associate grapheme and phoneme decreases the efficiency of their explicit phonological processing of oral language. 'The missing of a single skill (grapheme–phoneme association) interferes significantly in the higher development of the language system' (Reis and Castro-Caldas 1997: 449).

Adults' level of alphabetic literacy has been shown to affect a wide range of phonological skills, as well as verbal and visual memory, and visuospatial skills (Dellatolas, Braga, Souza, Filho, Queiroz, and Deloche 2003).[3] The participants in this study in Brazil were 97 illiterate adults and 41 children (ages 7–8). The measure of degree of literacy of all the participants was their ability to read sixteen short words and identify capital letters and numbers. The 'non-reader' group consisted of those who could not read a single word, and the 'reader' group was made up of those who could read at least one word. Each participant in the study took twenty tests, consisting of measures of word and non-word repetition, semantic and phonological fluency, rhyme identification, initial phoneme deletion, and memory span tests. The results of this study were the same as those reported in the studies above. Literate participants did significantly better than illiterate participants on phonological fluency and initial phoneme deletion tasks. A stepwise regression analysis showed that scores on four measures would accurately identify 86.8 percent of the participants as either readers or non-readers: phonological fluency, initial phoneme deletion, visual recognition, and digit span. The ability to name letters was significantly related to phonological fluency and initial phoneme deletion. Illiterate participants did not have difficulty with oral repetition in general, but they did have greater difficulty than literate participants in repeating long pseudowords. Dellatolas et al. (2003) suggest that the ability to repeat long pseudowords is important in learning new vocabulary items. A pseudoword, they suggest, can be viewed in the same way as any word an individual does not know the meaning of. In learning the meaning of a new long word, the individual must be able to hold the long word he or she does not understand in short-term memory, while asking or searching for its meaning.

These studies in the field of cognitive psychology and neuropsychology document the impact of literacy on the ability of adults to perform certain oral language-processing tasks, tasks that some may previously have assumed were universally accessible to mature adults. Surprisingly, these studies suggest that the ability to process oral language in terms of linguistic units rather than in terms of semantics is not innate. Rather, grapheme–phoneme correspondence (and the related abstract concept of 'word') appears to be the essential cognitive tool that enables human beings to focus on certain kinds of language form rather than only on semantics in the processing of oral language.

A broadening agenda for first language acquisition research

There is recent evidence that the fields of child L1 acquisition and child L1 reading research are expanding their related agendas to include the study of the relationship between children's oral language processing and acquisition, and their acquisition of literacy skills. It is well known that there is a large, specific set of syntactic structures that are characteristic of written, academic language, but not spoken language; most recently, Biber (1998) and Biber et al. (2002) have specified the syntactic differences between academic written and spoken English through corpus analysis. Ravid and Tolchinsky (2002) issued a position paper in the *Journal of Child Language* that proposes a new construct of 'linguistic literacy', which is defined as 'a constituent of language knowledge characterized by the availability of multiple linguistic resources and by the ability to consciously access one's own linguistic knowledge and to view language from various perspectives' (pp. 419–20). Rhetorical flexibility, or adaptability, is a key property of linguistic literacy. This flexibility is the ability to vary one's linguistic output in relation to different addressees and contexts, as well as the ability to create linguistic representations that can be manipulated for metalinguistic reflection. (The latter is the same ability that is the focus of the research we have just reviewed.) Linguistic literacy is acquired relatively late by school-age learners, at the same time as they add the major linguistic modality of writing to their earlier-acquired modality of speech. As the cognitive researchers we have reviewed above have also concluded, Ravid and Tolchinsky argue that it is in the process of learning to read and write that school-age learners become more aware of language itself.

For Ravid and Tolchinsky (2002), the construct of linguistic literacy has two dimensions: discourse[4] and notational code. The discourse dimension relates to the increasingly varied discourse styles acquired by the learner.[5] The notational code dimension, for English, is an alphabetic system, which requires that four types of knowledge systems be mastered: phonology (grapho-phonemic relationship); orthography (fonts, upper/lower case), morpho-phonology (emic/etic distinctions like flap /t/ in American English 'butter'); and morphology (past tense marker in English). To learn these four systems, the individual must construct an internal model of the units of spoken language that are represented by the features of the written script. For example, punctuation involves marking word boundaries and sentence boundaries. Ravid and Tolchinsky (2002: 430) state:

> Written text conventions promote metalinguistic thinking in various
> linguistic domains such as sound/letter correspondence, word and
> sentence boundaries, and appropriate grammatical constructions (e.g.
> past perfect in English, passé simple in French, or optional bound
> morphology in Hebrew). . . . the reciprocal character of speech and writing
> in a literate community makes it a synergistic system where certain
> features (e.g. basic syntax) originate in the spoken input, while others,
> such as complex syntax and advanced and domain-specific lexical items,
> originate in the written input. Together, however, they form a 'virtual
> loop' where speech and writing constantly feed and modify each other.

In exactly the same way that Dellatolas and colleagues speculated above, Ravid and Tolchinsky conclude that speakers of a language who are not alphabetically literate must necessarily focus on the meaning of their utterances, and not upon the linguistic form of their language. But individuals who are becoming alphabetically literate begin to develop an explicit and analytical awareness of language itself. And with that awareness, argue Ravid and Tolchinsky, comes increasing cognitive control. Cognitive links are established between the internal representation of phonemes, syllables, and morphemes and their written representations, and these newly articulated representations become the locus of increasing control in the cognition of the individual.

The Ravid and Tolchinsky (2002) paper appears with ten response papers from leading scholars on child L1 development (e.g. Berman 2002; Biber et al. 2002; Verhoeven 2002). The responses of these scholars suggest that there is substantial support for Ravid and Tolchinsky's new construct. For example, Kail (2002) points out that the construct can help explain patterns of French L1 acquisition. In French, there is considerable discontinuity between the oral and written code, as, for example, in verbal number agreement: *fille/filles*, *il chante/ils chantent*. Children learning French initially just use word order as a basis for their sentence interpretations, and do not add morphology as a factor until much later. Scholars studying the acquisition of French as an L1 have been unable to say what it is that causes French children to start to use morphology to interpret oral input. Kail (2002: 465) states:

> the developmental change in French children's processing could be explained by their increasing mastery of morphological cues supplied by growing knowledge of the written code which is clearer and more regular than the oral one. It seems reasonable to assume that linguistic literacy makes French morphology more accessible and more consistent providing a stable representation for agreements ... we have to predict that literacy may cause the child to notice conflict cases in the input (for example, between word order and morphology) she has never noticed before.

Similarly, Jim Miller (2002) considers the implications for innatist views of child language acquisition of the notion that linguistic literacy is a skill that is dependent on learning to read and write. For example, researchers know that complex syntactic structures such as the full relative clause system in English are acquired very late. Miller (2002: 473) points out that nativist theories of language acquisition

> assume a large endowment of innate linguistic knowledge, without which it would (allegedly) be impossible for children to acquire the complex structures of any language. Once the complexities of written language are seen as learned over a longish period of schooling, once spontaneous spoken language is recognized as being relatively simple and once it is recognized that children do receive negative evidence (Sokolov and Snow 1994), nativist theories lose their *raisons d'être*. This is the most important consequence of paying attention to literacy and the distinction between spoken and written language.

Thus, researchers and scholars in the different fields of child language acquisition and adult cognitive processing are all converging on the conclusion that the acquisition of literacy in an alphabetic language significantly changes human beings' oral processing of language, enabling them to focus on and manipulate language in terms of its metalinguistic form rather than solely in terms of its semantics.

Olson (2002: 164) argues that such findings support the view that literacy is in fact what makes metalinguistic awareness possible.

> Writing is what introduces our speech to us, revealing our speech as having a particular structure. Children do not know that they speak words, that is, that the flow of speech can be thought of as a string of lexical items. But children in an alphabetic society do come to think about language, minds, and world in terms of the category systems employed in writing. To paraphrase Whorf (1956), we dissect language along lines laid down by our scripts.

Perhaps the most startling claim Olson makes has immediate implications for SLA researchers studying explicit versus implicit language processing and the impact of corrective feedback. According to Olson (2002), our very ability to correct the grammatical errors of others is inextricably tied to our literacy; our notions of prescriptive grammar, used to correct ourselves and others, come from standards acquired in reading and writing. 'With writing, editing becomes inevitable' (Olson 2002: 162).

Summary

In this chapter, we have described research with native language speakers on the relationship between two abilities: the ability to decode alphabetic print script, and the ability to perform oral phonological awareness tasks. Phonological awareness is measured by oral tasks requiring the manipulation of language units such as phonemes, syllables, and words. The research we have presented shows that alphabetic print literacy (specifically, grapheme–phoneme correspondence) is a skill that significantly improves the ability of both children and adults explicitly to process and manipulate units of oral language in this way.

Research with child literacy has long established that there is a close relationship between alphabetic print literacy and phonological awareness. But, because these two skills develop at virtually the same time in children, the directionality of the relationship has been impossible to establish. The research of cognitive psychologists comparing literate and illiterate adults is particularly important, because it can help to establish the directionality of the relationship between literacy and phonological awareness. The studies reviewed in this chapter compared illiterate adults with literate adults who were closely matched with them in terms of life experience, age, and a wide range of other individual variables, with the only variable distinguishing these two groups being literacy. These studies showed that the performance of these two groups differed significantly on phonological processing tasks that required an awareness of linguistic segments such as phonemes. Such studies provide evidence of the directionality of the relationship between literacy and phonological awareness. It is the acquisition of the ability to decode an alphabetic script that enables the individual to do oral language tasks requiring an awareness of and ability to manipulate linguistic units. Research on L1 acquisition supports this conclusion, documenting the longitudinal impact of reading and writing on the development of linguistic literacy and the acquisition of the more complex aspects of the native language rule system. Alphabetic literacy thus promotes the acquisition of linguistic skills previously assumed by language researchers and theoreticians to be innate, making possible explicit (as opposed to implicit) oral language processing, and altering the structure of the individual's short-term memory for oral language.

In Chapter 2, we will explore in detail the implications of these findings for current research on SLA.[6]

Notes

1. The autonomous model of literacy (Street 1993a) is one in which sets of competences are framed as separate from the situations in which they are used.
2. This is not to say that adults do not develop or lose certain cognitive processes, but the changes are not as dramatic as the processes children go through during the time they are typically learning to read.
3. The results of this study are also reported in Loureiro et al. (2004).
4. In the discourse dimension, linguistic literacy makes variability (both user-related and context-dependent variation) accessible and controllable. It enables the language user to increase his or her control over register (distinctions that express social dimensions such as power, authority, distance, politeness), genre (text types defined by function, communicative purpose, and sociocultural practice), and modality (oral versus writing, with its lack of audience, stable language signal, more control over linguistic output).
5. Here Ravid and Tolchinsky rely heavily on the work of Biber and his colleagues (Biber 1988; Biber and Hared 1991), who show that the registers of oral and written language are basically different, and that the syntactic constructions used in written registers are typically more complex and the information structure of written registers more dense.
6. An earlier version of Chapter 1 appeared in Tarone and Bigelow (2005).

2

SLA research with low-literate learners

Low literacy among adolescents and adults

Worldwide there are about 774 million adults who lack minimum literacy skills. One in five adults is still not literate, and two-thirds of these are women. In addition, there are 72.1 million children in the world who are not attending school and many more who attend irregularly or drop out.[1]

Many of these illiterate individuals are L2 learners. Despite their limited literacy, as Hill (1970) points out, people around the world learn not only one, but often two or more languages. In the USA, adolescent immigrant and refugee English-language learners with limited or interrupted formal schooling have become a critical mass. Even in the early 1990s, Fleischman and Hopstock (1993) found that 20 percent of English-language learners at the secondary-school level and 12 percent of children between the ages of 11 and 14 had missed two or more years of schooling since the age of 6. In 2001, among Hispanic students age 15–17 who were newcomers, more than one-third were enrolled below the level that corresponds to their age and were not literate in Spanish (Jamieson, Curry, and Martinez 2001). Short and Fitzsimmons (2007: 15) cite dramatic National Assessment for Educational Progress figures that indicate that there is nothing less than a 'literacy crisis for English language learners', a literacy crisis where 96 percent of students with limited English proficiency beginning secondary school score below the basic level and 31 percent fail to complete secondary school. They conclude: 'Adolescent English language learners with limited formal schooling and below-grade-level literacy are most at risk of educational failure' (Short and Fitzsimmons 2007: 16).

Illiterate adult L2 learners are also common in the USA. McHugh, Gelatt, and Fix (2007) estimate that approximately 750,000 adult immigrants in the United States are not literate in English or their native language(s). Their results are compiled in Table 2.1, showing how this population, which was classified as 'Level 0' out of six possible levels of L2 English proficiency, is spread across age groups.

Age	Authorized Immigrants	
	Number	**Percentage of all immigrants**
56+	162,159	15
50–55	39,025	10
25–49	178,394	5
17–24	17,800	2
	Unauthorized Immigrants	
	Number	**Percentage of all immigrants**
25+	311,069	6
17–25	39,304	3

Source: McHugh, Gelatt, and Fix (2007). MPI analysis of tabulations of 2000 census data and 2005 CPS with imputations of legal status by the Urban Institute.

Table 2.1 Number of authorized and unauthorized immigrants in the United States by age who are likely to have limited formal schooling and low literacy, 2000 and 2005

Very early in our field, Jane Hill (1970) urged SLA researchers for failing to theorize about L2 learning that occurs among unschooled and illiterate learners in places where multilingualism is the norm. Yet, in the intervening decades of scholarly work, SLA researchers have not singled out for study L2 learners who are illiterate or have low literacy levels. As a result, we do not know how literacy level affects the acquisition of oral L2s.

In this chapter, we argue that SLA research must expand to include the study of the impact of alphabetic literacy on oral processes of SLA. Quite apart from the practical need, we suggest that an adequate theory of SLA, one that describes and explains the *human* capacity for SLA, should include the learning experiences of illiterate and low-literate learners. Much can be learned from the study of the oral abilities of such L2 learners.

In Chapter 1, we reviewed the work of researchers and scholars who have examined the relationship between the acquisition of literacy in an alphabetic script and the ability to process oral language in terms of the formal linguistic segments encoded in that script. In this chapter, we consider the implications of the scholarly findings reviewed in Chapter 1 for some of the most central constructs in SLA research: awareness and the noticing hypothesis, short-term memory, implicit and explicit learning, corrective feedback, and developmental stages of acquisition.

Literacy, awareness, and the noticing hypothesis

An early definition of the noticing hypothesis in SLA (Schmidt 1990) posited that L2 learners must consciously notice a linguistic form in order to acquire it. Noticing is defined as a conscious focus on 'elements of the surface structure of utterances in the input' (Schmidt 2001: 5). An L2 learner can notice these elements in several ways: through L2 output or L2 input, or through interaction with others using the L2. Noticing may or may not result in acquisition, but Schmidt's hypothesis says that every L2 linguistic form that is acquired has to have been noticed, at some point in time. There is considerable debate in the field, however, about this assertion. Even those who accept the view that noticing is essential in SLA may disagree about how explicit this noticing of L2 elements must be and what tools learners must access to leverage noticing into acquisition. The research reviewed in Chapter 1 bears directly upon this disagreement.

Schmidt (1990, 1993, 1994b, 1995a) has persistently argued that awareness at the level of noticing (conscious attention) is necessary and sufficient for language learning to occur and that this process is central to all areas of SLA. SLA researchers who study noticing posit that, when learners are exposed to L2 input, they are able to select only portions of the input that they can subsequently convert into intake. It is this portion of the input that is consciously noticed. However, how much attention is required in SLA noticing? The question is widely debated among researchers (Sharwood Smith 1981, 1991; Schmidt 1990, 1993, 1994a, 1995b, 2001; Long 1991; R. Ellis 1993; Tomlin and Villa 1994). For example, Schmidt distinguishes between two levels of awareness. The first is awareness at the level of *noticing* and the second is awareness at the level of *understanding*. Schmidt (1993: 26) explains that noticing involves 'registering the simple occurrence of some event, whereas understanding implies recognition of a general principle, rule, or pattern' and argues that 'noticing is crucially related to the question of what linguistic material is stored in memory'.

Another group of researchers differs from Schmidt in the role they accord to noticing in the process of SLA. Tomlin and Villa (1994) argue for a more fine-grained functional analysis of attention, consisting of the attentional functions of *alertness*, *orientation*, and *detection*. Tomlin and Villa predict that alertness and orientation may or may not be present for detection to occur, but still argue that detection is essential for SLA.

And, of course, there are still others (Krashen 1981, 1982, 1985, 1994; Paradis 1994; Zobl 1995) who argue that there may be two learning systems at work, one completely conscious (learning) and the other completely unconscious (acquisition). Certainly these SLA theorists in particular would have no problem explaining findings that low-literate and illiterate adults succeed in acquiring L2s with minimal noticing or analysis of L2 linguistic forms. The learning process Schmidt describes requires a conscious apprehension and awareness of input, and a fairly explicit internalization of the linguistic form that was noticed. But certain qualities of the linguistic form may make that form more or less noticeable. For instance, some linguistic items are too rare, abstract, complex, or semantically opaque, or have too many irregularities to be explicitly noticeable by learners. The article system in English is a typical problem for learners of many different native languages. But the fact that learners with no apparent metalinguistic knowledge are often successful with complex linguistic structures such as the English article system suggests that implicit learning can occur in such cases. Indeed, with low-literate adolescents and adults, this type of implicit learning of L2 systems may be the norm.

With regard to noticing and awareness, then, we have seen that Schmidt (1990) and others claim that *conscious noticing* of features of the L2 is necessary for L2 learning to take place. On the other hand, Krashen and others argue that there are two learning systems at work, one more implicit and the other more explicit, and that, for at least one of these learning systems, this kind of conscious awareness is not necessary, and can even inhibit the process.

The work just reviewed in Chapter 1 raises some troubling questions for the noticing hypothesis and these positions on awareness. Research on literacy shows that an individual's awareness of linguistic forms is not innate. Rather, this research shows conclusively that the ability to process language explicitly in terms of its phonological form is a product of acquiring alphabetic literacy. So how do illiterate older learners acquire L2s if they do not consciously notice linguistic units, and if they process language semantically and implicitly rather than explicitly and in terms of linguistic representations? Is it possible that the noticing hypothesis applies only to *literate* L2 learners? Since we have not tested it with data from illiterate L2 learners, we do not know.

If L2 learners who are not literate in any language do not consciously notice segmental linguistic forms in oral input in the L2 (a reasonable assumption, given that the research shows they do not notice them in their native language), then the SLA noticing hypothesis would predict that learners who do not notice linguistic segments cannot acquire an L2 at all. And yet, as Jane Hill told us in 1970, it is clear that many illiterate adults worldwide do acquire L2s through oral input. We see in our immigrant populations that illiterate Latino, Hmong, and Somali adults do become fluent in oral English, their L2.

What are the theoretical implications of these facts? One possibility is that the ability to consciously notice and analyze oral L2 input in terms of segmental linguistic units holds only for alphabetically literate L2 learners, but not for illiterate ones. Thus, illiterate adults may retain the ability to internalize the L2 unconsciously, in the same way they internalized their L1. But, once adults become literate, this may change the way they internalize L2s; now they must consciously notice an L2 structure to internalize it. This possibility is quite global: illiterate adults acquire L2s (in Krashen's 1982 sense) and literate adults tend to learn them.

A second possibility is that the noticing hypothesis does apply, but only to some linguistic forms of the L2 and not others. The Reis and Castro-Caldas (1997) model, reviewed in Chapter 1, suggests that both semantic and phonological processing strategies may be in play at the same time, and findings of subsequent studies (e.g. Kosmidis, Tsapkini, Folia, Vlahou, and Kiosseoglou 2004) have supported this view. In other words, a core set of syntactic structures used in the spoken L2 may be acquirable unconsciously, with semantic processing, and not require noticing of linguistic form. If this is true, an illiterate L2 learner may become quite proficient in the oral use of these structures, without ever noticing them. Other syntactic and morphological forms may not be learned by such a learner, because those forms require noticing. This possibility may be supported by Ravid and Tolchinsky (2002), reviewed in Chapter 1. These scholars might suggest that full mastery of the syntactic structures characteristic of the written L2, as well as of linguistic literacy in the L2, may require conscious attention and noticing. This could mean that the noticing hypothesis may apply only or primarily to the acquisition of that set of complex syntactic structures that characterize written language: that is, it may apply primarily or only to the acquisition of linguistic literacy in the L2.

The role of literacy level in fostering awareness and noticing of L2 forms in the input, including in corrective feedback, has not been explored. We need to include illiterate and low-literate adult L2 learners in research on noticing, attention, and awareness in SLA. The possibilities raised in the paragraph above are surely all researchable hypotheses. To our knowledge, the acquisition/learning hypothesis has never been tested in a population of completely illiterate L2 learners, in order to identify the impact of literacy on acquisition versus learning in SLA. This would seem to be an important study just waiting to be done. In the same way, a population of illiterate L2 learners would seem to be ideal for testing the hypothesis that noticing applies more to some linguistic forms than to others, and, if so, which L2 forms need to be noticed to be learned, and which ones do not. It is not known whether, or the degree to which, literacy affects L2 learners' ability to notice given features in L2 input. It is not known whether literacy affects the noticing of grammatical forms that are easier for an L2 student to read than to hear (for example, the grammatical morphemes that mark regular past-tense endings, third-person singular and plural –s). It is not known how literacy affects noticing of corrective feedback on such forms. All the evidence on whether recasts, for example, can promote noticing comes from literate, if not privileged, L2 learners.[2] The results of all SLA studies of learners with minimal literacy should have important implications for pedagogy in adolescent and adult L2 literacy programs.

Literacy and short-term memory

We will discuss the impact of literacy on short-term and working memory in some depth in Chapter 5. For now, we will simply point out that current models of speech processing proposed in Baddeley (1986, 2003, 2007), Levelt (1992) and Randall (2007) suggest that the role of memory in SLA is likely to be more complex than Schmidt's noticing hypothesis suggests: auditory input must be decoded and processed, which involves short-term memory;

comprehension and comparison involve both short-term and long-term memory; and past learning (memory) may influence perception itself. Levelt's model illustrates this well. Working within Levelt's model, we might say that, when an L2 learner responds to corrective feedback in a recast study, linguistic input can result in acquisition. This process requires more than just attending to the 'surface elements' of the input, as Schmidt (2001) claims above. The process begins when the learner perceives the input via acoustic decoding. Acoustically processed input moves into the short-term store, where it can undergo comprehension or learning processes. During comprehension, the input is parsed by processes that use as resources multiple types of knowledge, both semantic and metalinguistic. At this point, restructuring of the mental representation of interlanguage knowledge may occur. New form-meaning mappings may be created and existing mappings refined, so that cognitive comparisons and other internal representations can be made.

We wonder, however, if L2 learners with minimal alphabetic literacy (learners who, like the adults in the studies described in Chapter 1, lack print literacy) are as efficient as literate learners are in processing recasts and producing target-like reformulations. Their working memory may not hold competing utterances in storage in a way that lets them compare linguistic forms. This ability to zero in on specific contrasting elements of language form is what is needed to enable learners to select only portions of the input that they can subsequently convert into intake.

It must be stressed here that a great deal of oral language acquisition clearly occurs without the assistance to short-term memory that is provided by alphabetic print literacy. Illiterate individuals, both children and adults, acquire a lot of language via the oral modalities, in both their native and their second languages. However, it is increasingly probable that literate and illiterate individuals process oral language differently, using different cognitive processes to acquire oral L2s.

Literacy, and implicit and explicit learning

We have mentioned the view of SLA researchers such as Krashen, Paradis, and Zobl that L2 learners may internalize the L2 either explicitly or implicitly, and may also employ two knowledge systems, one implicit and one explicit. DeKeyser and Juffs (2005: 437) include both possibilities in their review of cognitive considerations in L2 learning, stating:

> Learners acquire some specific knowledge about the structure of L2 explicitly (with concurrent awareness of what is being learned) and some implicitly (without such awareness).

Bialystok (1981) characterizes explicit knowledge as knowledge that is analyzed and understood independently of its application. She argues that explicit knowledge has a conscious representation, and that, if asked, an L2 learner would be able to say what it is that he or she knows. Conversely, implicit knowledge is unanalyzed and unavailable for report. In this section, we explore further the claims that have been made for implicit versus explicit language processing in SLA.

There is a considerable body of cross-disciplinary work on implicit and explicit learning, with potential to inform the study of L2 learners with limited print literacy. The broad field of implicit learning began with the work of Arthur Reber in 1967, according to Stadler and Frensch (1998: p. ix). Currently, implicit learning, teaching, memory, and knowledge are all researched widely in the various disciplines of psychology, linguistics, cognitive science, neuroscience, education, and philosophy. Reber presents a convincing case for the robustness of implicit cognitive processes over explicit cognitive processes. He bases his claims on, among other things, evidence that implicit processes tend to survive neurological and psychological trauma better than their explicit counterparts. Reber (supported by Carr and Curran (1994)) argues that the endurance of implicit learning in times of trauma to the brain is evidence for at least some degree of dissociation between the two systems of explicit and implicit learning. Although Reber (1993: 25) presents a strong case for what he calls 'the primacy of the implicit... the default mode for the acquisition of complex information about the environment', he concedes that it is important

> not to treat implicit and explicit learning as though they were completely separate and independent processes; they should properly be viewed as interactive components or cooperative processes, processes that are engaged in what Mathews (1991: 23) likes to call a 'synergistic' relationship.

Reber (1993) hypothesizes that implicit systems have other qualities, in addition to robustness. He believes that they are age independent and show few effects on developmental stage; that they have low rates of variability in terms of population or individual-to-individual variation; that implicit systems are independent of so-called intelligence assessment tools, and that implicit learning 'should show cross-species commonality' (p. 88). Current research on attention and awareness in cognitive neuroscience can be argued to support Reber's view that implicit systems of cognition are omnipresent (e.g. Soon et al. 2008).

Anderson's Adaptive Control Theory (ACT) (1982) explores the automatization of the learner's access to information along a continuum. (The terms often used, both by Anderson and Bialystok, are *procedural* (automatized) and *declarative* (not automatized) knowledge.) Anderson argues that all interesting complex human skills begin with labored, conscious, and overtly controlled (that is, explicit) processes and gradually give way to smooth and covertly controlled (that is, implicit) processes. This approach would seem to be at odds with Reber's focus on implicit learning, because it assumes that knowledge begins in an explicit form and gradually moves to the implicit form. However, Reber (1993) relegates this type of knowledge to skill learning, and thus argues that the ACT is not at odds with his notions of implicit learning. In a revised version of his theory (ACT-R), Anderson states that skilled behavior can be either rule based or instance based, and neither is carried out without awareness.

The work of Reber, Mathews, Anderson, and others, focused on the power of implicit cognitive systems, is quite interesting in the light of the current assumption apparent in a large body of recent SLA research that explicit language processing is central. Doughty and Williams (1998a), R. Ellis (2002), Long and Robinson (1998), and Norris and Ortega (2000, 2001) all conclude from reviews of the research that has been conducted to date (all of which, of course, was carried out with L2 learners who are literate) that these support the importance of explicit learning. An important question for all these scholars, however, is the question of how implicit L2 cognitive systems evolve from explicit L2 learning. That is, how does explicit knowledge become automatized? DeKeyser and Juffs (2005) conclude that this is far from clear.

Another key question for our present discussion in relation to explicit versus implicit L2 learning is whether low-literate or illiterate adult L2 learners process L2 input explicitly or implicitly. Do illiterate or low-literate L2 learners also begin with explicit processing in the way SLA researchers have shown that literate L2 learners do? Or do they internalize L2 knowledge more implicitly, moving it directly into an indirect knowledge base? We do not know, because this research has not been done.

Literacy and corrective feedback

A strand of current SLA research focuses on learners' ability to benefit from corrective feedback. Corrective feedback is a response to learner utterances that contain an error. Such feedback may provide any or all of these three elements: an indication that an error has been committed, the correct target language form, or metalinguistic information about the error's nature (Ellis, Loewen, and Erlam 2006). When a learner produces an erroneous L2 form, as in (a) below, a teacher may model the correct target language form using a recast, as in (b) below.

(a) *What color *it is*?
(b) What color *is it*?

In this case, if the L2 learner who produced (a) is to benefit from the corrective feedback in (b), he or she must *notice* the correct L2 form in (b), compare it with the learner language form in (a), and then incorporate (b) in place of (a). Nelson (1987), R. Ellis (1994: 95–6), and Saxton (1997) refer to the entire process of noticing, comparison, and incorporation described above as *cognitive comparison*.

It is believed that corrective feedback gives L2 learners opportunities to make cognitive comparisons, receive negative and positive evidence, notice syntactic or lexical gaps in the L2, and in general negotiate both form and meaning with native or nonnative interlocutors (e.g. Chun, Day, Chenoweth, and Luppescu 1982; Gass 1985). Nelson (1987) and Saxton (1997) have argued that cognitive comparison requires the ability to hold both the initial utterance and the corrective feedback in the short-term memory long enough for the individual to examine the initial utterance against the negative evidence. These comparisons should ultimately result in uptake: the incorporation of the correct form or rule into the L2 learner's long-term memory, or the formation of a new rule in the learner's interlanguage. It is this kind of cognitive comparison process in which L2 learners are assumed to engage after they experience pedagogical interventions using any of several focus-on-form techniques (Doughty and Williams 1998a) intended to direct or attract their attention to a new or problematic form in the L2. Noticing, the implicit–explicit continuum, and memory theories in SLA are thus intertwined and ripe for investigation with understudied populations and such individual variables as limited formal schooling and low literacy.

One area of corrective feedback that is of particular interest to researchers and practitioners is the use of recasts in oral interaction (e.g. Lyster and Ranta 1997; Long, Inagaki, and Ortega 1998; Lyster 2004; Ammar and Spada 2006; Carpenter, Jeon, MacGregor, and Mackey 2006; Ellis and Sheen 2006; Loewen and Philp 2006; McDonough and Mackey 2006; Egi 2007). Recasts, which provide an immediate correct reformulation of an L2 learner's erroneous utterance, can direct learner attention to non-target components of their speech at moments when they are focused on meaning. Recasts can provide a very effective way to help these literate learners make form–meaning connections that will help them acquire the L2. Nevertheless, L2 learners do not always notice, or may misinterpret the intended focus of, the recast (Lyster 1998b, c; Mackey, Gass, and McDonough 2000; Carpenter et al. 2006). Research with these L2 learners suggests that their failure to notice seems to have been due to such factors as their proficiency level, their metalinguistic skills, or qualities of the recast such as its explicitness, length, or complexity (for example, the number of lexical or syntactic changes in the recast to the original utterance).

If the findings reported in Chapter 1 documenting the impact of literacy on native language oral processing are accurate, then L2 learners who are illiterate or even those who have low levels of literacy may find it more difficult to notice oral corrective feedback and to perform cognitive comparisons in working memory. Because they do not have literacy-based tools for working memory, tools described by Reis and Castro-Caldas (1997: 445) as 'strategies for dealing with oral language: that is, conscious phonological processing, visual formal lexical representation, and all the associations that these strategies allow', then illiterate and low-literate L2 learners who are provided with oral corrective feedback may find it more difficult to notice it, accurately identify its formal focus in relation to their own erroneous output, and otherwise engage the process of cognitive comparison.

Literacy and the order of acquisition in SLA

SLA research has identified a clear sequence of development for several L2 grammatical forms. Predictable sequences of development have been identified for L2 learners acquiring, for example, negation or question formation in English. Yet, in the light of the research we have reviewed so far, we must remember that all the information we have on these sequences of development of L2s is derived from observation and study of literate L2 learners. Only two research projects, to our knowledge, have studied the order of acquisition in SLA of 'relatively uneducated' learners. The European Science Foundation (ESF) Project examined the SLA of working-class adult immigrants with 'limited education' (Perdue 1993); unfortunately, they did not, to our knowledge, establish how literate their 'limited-education' informants were. The second study of the SLA of working-class adult immigrants in Europe, the Zweitspracherwerb Italienischer und Spanischer Arbeiter (ZISA) project, identified invariant orders of acquisition based on word order that held for all the L2 learners in the study. But the ZISA researchers also identified two 'variational' acquisitional routes within this population. Although developmental interlanguage (IL) stages based on word order were the same for both groups (that is, were considered 'invariant'), there were also variational features that differentiated the two groups. Though all the L2 learners followed the same developmental stage in terms of L2 word order, the learners varied in the degree to which they supplied morphological features in their interlanguages. One group preferred a 'standard' orientation, which prioritized accuracy, while the other group had a 'simplifying' orientation, favoring communicative effectiveness (Clahsen, Meisel, and Pienemann 1983). In general, the first, 'elaborating', group supplied grammatical morphemes, while the second, 'simplifying', group tended to delete them.

Unfortunately, the ZISA study did not include any objective measure of literacy level in L1 or L2, and so we do not know whether literacy level was related to learners' 'simplifying' or 'elaborating' pathways of acquisition. While ZISA did record learners' self-reported educational levels, we know from Kosmidis et al. (2004) that educational level does not have the same effect on phonological awareness as literacy level. And, of course, it is possible to be relatively uneducated but still to be literate, and equally possible to report spending several years in school but not to be particularly literate. It would be interesting to know whether the L1 literacy levels of the adult immigrants in this study were related to the learners' preference for either an 'elaborating' or a 'simplifying' acquisitional path. There is good reason, as we have seen in Chapter 1, to expect that alphabetic print literacy should help L2 learners to notice and process linguistic units that do not carry semantic meaning: units like grammatical morphemes. Low-literate and illiterate L2 learners will be more likely to use semantic processing, thus gravitating to a 'simplifying' acquisitional path.

A second area for exploration has to do with the developmental stages themselves. The cognitive processing strategies that underlie the stages of acquisition in the Multidimensional Model/Processability Theory are argued to be universal: the same across all L2 learners (see Meisel, Clahsen, and Pienemann 1981; Clahsen et al. 1983; Pienemann and Johnston 1987). These stages are based on the way in which learners in these studies have processed word order in the L2. But the claim of universality should be tested with L2 learners whom we *know* to be illiterate and low literate. Neither literacy, nor the phonological awareness that it confers, is innate. Does alphabetic literacy alter the 'universal' word order sequence predicted by Processability Theory? Do illiterate adults follow the same stages of acquisition as literate adults? If not, what does this tell us about human language processing in SLA? Space does not permit us to explore such implications in this chapter, but we hope that others will take up such considerations in future publications. Future longitudinal studies of SLA among populations of adult immigrants should use objective measures of L1 and L2 literacy levels, and seek to identify correlations between scores on those measures and developmental paths in SLA.

Summary

We have argued in Chapter 2 that the SLA research agenda needs to be more inclusive in terms of recognizing the multiple conditions in which L2 learning occurs and the multiple characteristics learners bring to the enterprise. We have argued that SLA researchers should study L2 learners who are not literate in either their L1 or their L2. It is imperative that the learners we describe in this book become part of the mainstream SLA research agenda if we are fully to understand the way key variables affect SLA processes throughout the world.

The findings and considerations we review here present a major challenge to several SLA theories. SLA theorists routinely make generalizations about SLA that may not apply to L2 learners with interrupted educational experiences or low levels of literacy. While we have made some hypotheses above about how literacy level may affect some key areas of SLA, these hypotheses need to be carefully tested. Although it will take considerable effort to include them, the study of less-educated, less-literate L2 learners will contribute to SLA theory-building. Most importantly, as we have argued above, it will show us how our own literacy may bias our perceptions as researchers. In this way, research with this unstudied population will broaden our view of the nature of SLA and of the human potential for language learning. And, finally, the results of this research will be most welcome throughout the world in classrooms where illiterate and low-literate learners are struggling to acquire an L2, often in societal systems where their life chances crucially depend upon their success.

Notes

1 See http://portal.unesco.org/education/ for worldwide and national literacy statistics.
2 For examples, see Doughty and Williams (1998b), Mackey (1999), Izumi and Bigelow (2000), and Philp (2003).

3
Methodology

This chapter will lay out our methodological stance, our procedures for participant recruitment, a description of our participants, and a description of all of our instrumentation (that is, tests, tasks, and their respective protocols). We are committed to research in understudied populations: understudied because of their culture, language, or educational backgrounds. It is our strong belief that any work within such populations requires building relationships in their communities and not leaving participants feeling exploited or mystified by their interaction with us. In this chapter, we describe how we built relationships within the Somali community, using a methodology that we felt fit the setting and the participants. We were entering a community and culture we were just getting to know. We wished to proceed respectfully and in ways that would allow us to conduct our project ethically and not compromise access for future university researchers.

SLA research in a refugee community

Recruitment cannot rely on written notices; the less-literate population must be reached through personal contacts in the community. The willingness of unschooled learners to participate in a study may be moderated by an understandable skepticism of the purpose of university-sponsored research and distrust of researchers who do not belong to their community. Any Internal Review Board for research should have serious concerns about the ability of researchers to obtain informed consent from immigrant/refugee adults or adolescents with low levels of literacy. Obtaining informed consent from participants for an SLA study is relatively unproblematic with educated adults studying a language at a university who may have participated in studies before and can clearly understand and dispute information on a consent form. However, obtaining informed consent from learners who are not literate is fraught with problems. Obtaining informed consent typically requires an interpreter/liaison from the participant's culture, who understands the world of the unschooled, yet can also understand the nature of the study and the terms of participation. While the magnitude of these issues may be common in anthropological or sociological research, SLA researchers have not typically been faced with such challenges.

Less-literate L2 learners may belong to traditional cultural groups that may feel uncomfortable with a number of practices that are considered routine in SLA. For example, while we know that various characteristics of the interlocutor always make a difference in the type and quality of language that we are able to elicit from L2 learners, the gender of the researcher for some participants may render data collection completely impossible. Another example is the use of audio and videotaping equipment, which we know can be obtrusive under any circumstances, but in some cultures are completely taboo.

Our point is simply that researchers cannot assume that their participants will perceive their presence, their questions, their tasks, and their equipment as acceptable in the same way as participants from backgrounds comparable to that of the researcher. Thus, it seems that there are countless assumptions that must be re-examined by researchers, most of whom are not members of these immigrant/refugee populations themselves. Nothing, it appears, can be unquestioned when we move out of the walls of academe to do SLA data collection among unschooled populations with radically different cultural backgrounds.

The Cedar Riverside neighborhood

The Minneapolis neighborhood in which much of the research in this book took place in 2004–5 is known as Cedar Riverside or the West Bank. It is located right next to one of the University of Minnesota's Twin Cities campuses. In the late 1890s, it was a thriving community of Scandinavian immigrants. More recently, the 2000 Census reported that 45 percent of the people then living in Cedar Riverside were foreign born. Cedar Riverside is not only a neighborhood of immigrants; it is a neighborhood of many *different* immigrant groups. The major population groups in the neighborhood are Somali, Oromo, Ethiopian, Hispanic, Vietnamese, and Korean.[1] The neighborhood is known as a center for the arts as well as for its large immigrant community, the largest in the Twin Cities. There is a community center that serves as a locus of day-to-day activities for youth (for example, basketball, homework help) and as a gathering place for elders and community groups. There are mosques, grocery stores that cater to the East African community, and many immigrant-owned restaurants and shops.[2] In the 2000 census, the population of the community was 7,545, and most of the adult population was between 18 and 24 years of age. Families with children made up 55 percent of the population, and most residents in the neighborhood rented, with a median monthly rental rate of $360 in 2000. The median income for the neighborhood in 1999 was $14,367, which is less than half of that for Minneapolis as a whole, and the labor force participation rate was 65 percent in 2000, which was 7 percentage points below the rate of the city of Minneapolis.[3]

A Somali journalist, M. M. Afrah (2004), portrays a visual image of the neighborhood: 'the Somali refugees in Minneapolis...made an unprecedented economic miracle and added color and extravaganza [to] hitherto sleepy neighborhoods.' He describes Somali malls

> that offer everything from Halaal meat to stylish leather shoes to men's and women's latest fashion, gold jewelry, money transfer or Xawaala offices, banners advertising the latest Somali movie, and video stores fully stocked with nostalgic love songs.

Afrah's description represents what others might term urban renewal, and he is accurate in that much of this renewal is due to immigrant and refugee business owners. The community also boasts a large number of Somali intellectuals and politicians—some say it is the largest such group in the world.

Brief background on the Somali community in Minnesota

Somalia (Soomaaliya) is in East Africa. The Somali people are a large ethnic group from the Horn of Africa. They live in Somalia, but their populations extend into Djibouti, Ethiopia, and Kenya, and now to large Diaspora communities throughout the world. Because of civil war[4] in Somalia, hundreds of thousands of Somalis[5] have been displaced, and now live all over the world. Official estimates of Somalis in Minnesota are between 10,000 and 25,000, but many believe the size of the population to be as high as 50,000.[6] Most official estimates of the size of immigrant communities in Minnesota name Latinos as the largest foreign-born group, numbering 175,000 in 2004, followed by approximately 60,000 Hmong.[7] This places Somalis as the third largest foreign-born group in Minnesota. The Minnesota Department of Education figures show that 9,583 children in the 2006/7 academic year reported speaking Somali as their primary home language. Again, to situate this number in the larger educational context in Minnesota, there were 32,239 children reporting Spanish as their primary home language and 22,665 children reporting Hmong as their primary home language in the same year. In Minnesota, Somalis follow an earlier massive Hmong refugee resettlement, which began in the 1970s. The Somalis have been the second largest refugee resettlement in the state.

To understand the meaning of this large migration of Somali refugees to a Midwestern American region, it is important to understand the larger picture. The total population of the state of Minnesota, according to 2006 Census, is 5,167,101.[8] The racial and ethnic make-up of the state and the cities where this research took place is shown in Table 3.1. Of those in the state who claimed a single racial identity, 87.8 percent were White (compared to 74% nationwide), 4.4 percent were Black or African American (compared to 12.4% nationwide),

Racial and ethnic make-up	United States	State of Minnesota	City of Minneapolis, MN	City of St Paul, MN
Claiming single racial identity as White	74	87.8	68.5	65.8
Claiming single racial identity as Black or African American	12.4	4.4	18.6	14.7
Claiming single racial category as Latino	14.8	3.9	4.9	8.6
Claiming single racial category as Asian	4.4	3.5	4.9	11.7
Speak a language other than English at home	19.7	9.6	19.3	22.9
Foreign born	12.5	6.6	14.8	13.8

Source: US Census, 2006.

Table 3.1 Racial and ethnic makeup of Minnesota, 2006 (%)

and 3.9 percent were Latino (compared to 14.8% nationwide). In the city of Minneapolis, the demographics were quite different from those in the wider state: 68.5 percent of the population said they were White, 18.6 percent said they were Black or African American, and 4.9 percent said they were Asian. In Minneapolis, 19.3 percent said they spoke a language other than English at home, which was comparable to the 19.7 percent nationwide, and 14.8 percent of the population was foreign born, compared to 12.5 percent nationwide. In the city of St Paul, 65.8 percent of the population said they were White, 14.7 percent said they were Black or African American, and 11.7 percent said they were Asian. In St Paul, 22.9 percent said they spoke a language other than English at home and 13.8 percent of the population was foreign born.

In Europe, Somalis are known to be the oldest African culture in London, with an estimated number of 65,000.[9] Although it is extremely difficult to obtain consistent and reliable figures about how many Somalis have migrated to North America, some have claimed that Toronto has the largest population of Somalis outside the East African region (Ethiopia; Kenya; Djibouti; Yemen). There are roughly 70,000 Somali immigrants living in Canada and about 23,000 residing in the Toronto Metropolitan Area (Kusow 2006). (Other estimates range from 65,000 to 90,000 Somali people in Toronto alone.[10])

Researchers' role and orientation in the Somali community

In any sort of research, qualitative or quantitative, a range of researcher identity markers inform hundreds of research decisions made from conceptualization to fruition of a study. All research has bias based on who the researcher is: his or her political orientation, religion, race, and age, among others. For this reason, it is important for the reader to know who we are and how we identify ourselves, in order better to understand the purpose of our research, its design, and how we analyzed our data.

All three primary researchers identify as female, White, and middle class. Religiously, we are within the dominant Judeo-Christian traditions in the United States. When we are treated as minorities, it is typically due to our gender. Tarone draws on her Scottish and Italian immigrant grandparents to define herself ethnically. Bigelow draws on her German and Irish heritage, or the myth of that heritage, to situate herself as a great-granddaughter of immigrants. Hansen, too, is of European—German, Danish, and Irish—heritage. We share an identity as advocates for immigrants, particularly in the realm of education. Our views are progressive, both with respect to immigrant policy (for example, we support amnesty for undocumented immigrants and would like to see the numbers of refugees resettled in the United States increase) and with respect to language policy (for example, we support multilingualism and multiculturalism). Our stance as educators and teacher educators is squarely within perspectives that promote culturally relevant pedagogy and additive bi/multilingualism.

A number of researchers carrying out ethnographic SLA research have stressed the importance of establishing a trusting relationship between the community being studied and the researcher (Duff and Early 1996; Rounds 1996; Blanco-Iglesias and Broner 1997; Duff 2002). It is important for the researcher to enter the community with care and respect, and to take the time to build mutual relationships of trust before initiating a study. Blanco-Iglesias and Broner, for example, took a year to build a relationship of trust with members of the community of the immersion school they studied, before ever beginning to gather data. The importance of this approach cannot be overemphasized, particularly when we do research in non-traditional social settings.

Although we had had extensive ESL teaching and cross-cultural experience, as well as experience in SLA research, we knew that possible participants in settings outside the University would be unlikely to know who we were. Members of the Somali community we might ask to work with us had no way of assessing our integrity and therefore no basis for agreeing to participate in our study. They knew no one from within their community who could give a character reference on our behalf. For this reason, we saw the need to establish our reputations in the Somali community so that we could build trust in the community prior to attempting to recruit participants. At the very beginning of our study, we had no idea what we did not know about doing research in community settings, in particular this community, and had no idea how involved we would get. Our early conceptualization of 'building trust' was admittedly instrumental; in order to get our data, we needed to work with participants in such a way that would make them want to come to our sessions and finish our battery of tests and tasks. What we found, however, was that our work in the community ended up going far beyond an instrumental trust-building activity for the purposes of data collection. We found ourselves immersed in a profound personal and professional development experience.

Our involvement began with participation in a community organization situated in one of the largely Somali immigrant neighborhoods where we wished to collect data. This involvement started more than a year prior to the date when we began collecting data. At the time we were working in the community, this organization, Family Opportunities for Literacy Collaborative, was led by a woman named Eileen Watson, who did community organizing: she ran meetings, invited and encouraged broad community participation, helped the group set goals, and applied for grants to fund their projects. The organization met in a community center in the neighborhood, which was located immediately adjacent to the West Bank campus of the University of Minnesota, where we had our offices. Many immigrant and refugee community members, including those who headed other community organizations, participated in the meetings and activities she organized. The focus of the organization's activities was on family literacy, health, and general well-being. As members of this organization, Hansen and Bigelow were particularly interested in working with the youth in the community. We assisted with homework-help programs (getting volunteers, disseminating information about the programs, and sharing this information among the various programs) and we also volunteered in these programs. Another project we worked on with youth leaders was organizing summer soccer programs for youth in the neighborhood (for example, finding places for the teams to practice, and recruiting coaches). Hansen volunteered for over a year teaching ESL literacy to adult Somalis through a related community organization. Bigelow served on the board of this organization for a number of years. Cumulatively, this ethnography-inspired 'non-research'-related work allowed us to get to know many people in the neighborhood, experience what everyday life in the community was like, and familiarize ourselves with the services, spaces, and people that could help us carry out our research. We argue that this work was absolutely essential to the study, not the least because what we learned informed our interactions with Somali immigrants and refugees throughout our research process.

In moving beyond the perimeter of our university campus, we instantly knew we were 'read' differently in this milieu, and, while we were eager to listen and learn, we were also given the opportunity at meetings to state, and perhaps even to assert, that we were from the university. We repeatedly said that we were interested in studying L2 learning, that we cared about immigrant education, and that we were concerned about Somali youth and young adults succeeding at school. While it was important for us to be transparent in our purposes for participating, the way we positioned ourselves in this new setting allowed us to announce our academic identity in order to be 'known' in this new setting in a similar way to that by which we were 'known' in our professional sphere among university students and colleagues. Our status, which we claimed through affiliation and profession, seemed to open doors for us, and our interests and expertise seemed to be welcomed. Likewise, members of the community organization and the wider community, who place a high value on education and teachers, seemed easily able to understand our role and interest in the community because of our repeated explanation of why we were interested. This is not to say that our budding reputation in the community always quelled suspicion or made the informed consent process any easier; however, this community engagement was an essential beginning, because it began to develop the kind of relationship we wanted to have with this community.

What we did not know at the beginning was how much we would learn and how much we did not know about Somali culture and the deep significance to the members of this Somali community of their immigration under circumstances of civil war, with its long delays in refugee camps. In the beginning, we learned simple, but important things. For example, we learned that being Somali usually means being Muslim. The period we had designated for data collection turned out to be, to our surprise, the holy month of Ramadan, when Muslims fast. Because of this, participants needed breaks at sundown to go and eat. We tried to schedule appointments early in the day, when they would have more energy. Sometimes, when our sessions lasted for quite a long time, our Muslim participants needed a break to pray. We had to be flexible.

Community liaison and participant recruitment

We learned that it was important to add to our research team a community liaison contact who understood and supported our research effort, and who could help us recruit appropriate participants, obtain informed consent, and ensure that participants arrived at the scheduled time and place. This is no small matter when working with adolescents and young adults with busy lives, often full of home and work responsibilities. We chose a young man who was a recent high-school graduate and a Somali refugee. He was recommended to us by a Somali community leader because he spoke English and Somali very well and was well known in the community among Somali adults and youth. He was an ideal liaison contact, because he spent much of his free time in the neighborhood, tutoring children at the homework-help centers and studying, worshiping, or socializing at the various mosques in the neighborhood. As per our agreement with our Internal Review Board of ethical practices in research at the University of Minnesota, we spent a great deal of time instructing our liaison contact how he was to present the research to potential participants. He was to look for Somali adolescents and young adults who had arrived within the past five years, had at least rudimentary English, and could meet us two or three times. We also coached him on how he was to facilitate the informed consent/assent[11] process for participants and their parents. He used a mobile phone to ensure that the researcher and the participant would converge at the agreed-upon time and place for the data collection to take place. He was paid for this work.

In the same way, the participants he brought us were paid a total of $45 for the sessions they did with us, with this amount paid incrementally at the end of each session: $10 for the first session, and the balance at the end of the second session unless another session was needed to complete the tasks, in which case the second payment was $15 and the last one $30. Participants were also paid an additional $10 if they referred an appropriate participant to us.

As our data collection progressed, we met many young people in the Somali community who entrusted us with their stories. We learned about their schooling experiences in the USA. They gave us their opinions about their teachers, their schools, and how they felt about themselves as students. One young man, after telling us (in fluent English) how he was failing in almost all his high-school classes, exclaimed that his American-born classmates 'have been doing Algebra since kindergarten!' Some participants compared their experiences in Minnesota to experiences they had had in other states and countries. One participant told us that San Diego was a much more integrated city than the cities in Minnesota. They talked about their religious study. One participant told us with pride that he no longer went to *dugsi* (Quranic school) because he had finished reading the whole Quran. He said his family was proud of him for this and that he was respected by his friends for this major accomplishment. These experiences drew us in and led to long-term mentoring and tutoring relationships and, for Bigelow, subsequent research projects that were qualitative and ethnographic in nature. She has pursued the topics of co-constructed racialized identity in an ethnographic interview study with thirty Somali adolescents (Bigelow 2008), and the role of social/cultural capital in the education of Somali youth (Bigelow 2007).

Research methodology

We chose an empirical and quantitative methodology for our first set of research studies in this community, which were intended, for the reasons laid out in the first chapters of this book, to explore the role of print literacy in L2 oral language production. We decided on a partial replication of Jenefer Philp's SLA study (1999, 2003) on learner processing of implicit negative feedback, which was carried out in an academic setting with highly literate participants. This study, published first as a dissertation and then in the journal *Studies in Second Language Acquisition*, was selected for several reasons. First, Philp's data were collected using only tasks in the oral mode; a surprising number of current SLA studies do not meet this criterion, requiring some degree of literacy. Secondly, we wanted our findings with this new and largely unstudied population to be relevant to SLA research issues of the day; Philp's study combined the research focuses of noticing, recasts, and interaction—all currently garnering attention among researchers in the field. Thirdly, we could easily adapt Philp's cross-sectional design; this was important, because this was our first foray into SLA inquiry with this population. We could certainly have chosen other studies or lines of research as our point of our departure for bringing this new population more fully into the SLA literature, but, for the reasons stated above, we chose Philp's.

We measured and quantified participants' levels of L1 and L2 literacy, and then, like Philp, we gathered and quantified L2 oral language data through a series of elicited interactive tasks. These tasks were designed to offer us a window into the participants' L2 oral language use at the time of the study, with literacy as the independent variable. We generated hypotheses about the relationship between literacy level and L2 oral skills and developed instruments and methods for measuring this relationship. We used alphabetic print literacy level as an independent variable and divided our participants into two groups based on their literacy-level scores, one with higher levels of literacy and one with lower levels of literacy.

We compared these two groups in terms of three analyses. First, we compared the relationship between their literacy level and their ability to notice recasts of their grammatical errors in question formation; this study is described in Chapter 4. We carried out two additional analyses. We compared the two literacy groups' ability to do oral elicited-imitation tasks as compared to their noticing of recasts; this analysis is described in Chapter 5. Finally, we described the grammatical forms the two literacy groups used in telling the same oral narrative; this analysis is presented in Chapter 6. We deductively analyzed our psychometric data for the recast and elicited-imitation analyses in Chapters 4 and 5 using both descriptive statistics and an inferential statistical method called exact permutation analysis, described in Chapter 4. In the study on recasts in Chapter 4, we followed up on our quantitative results with a qualitative description of the performance of one learner, examining his transcripts in detail, in order to identify features of discourse the participant did and did not attend to. These additional data enabled us to identify patterns and behaviors not predicted by our research questions in the quantitative study. To sum up, we characterized, exemplified, and analyzed learners' oral language production in relationship to their literacy level; while we offer examples from the data, our epistemological frame remains primarily quantitative in nature.

This descriptive analysis aims to identify synchronic patterns of L2 use. It cannot document second language development, because the participants were not followed over time. The inquiry simply describes participants' oral L2 use at a particular point in time in response to a predetermined set of elicitation tasks, and connects their quantified performance on these tasks with their scores on alphabetic print literacy measures.

Participants

Assessing alphabetic literacy level of participants

In order to determine whether there is a relationship between alphabetic print literacy level and the oral L2 skills participants have acquired, we need objective, reliable assessment instruments to measure both variables. Measures of L1 alphabetic literacy levels of speakers of common European languages do exist and have been used in studies on children's acquisition of English literacy skills (Verhoeven 1994). But similar measures appropriate for use with adults did not seem to exist in the USA. We sought to identify an assessment instrument capable of differentiating among very low levels of alphabetic print literacy in both Somali (L1) and English (L2). An extensive search of existing alphabetic literacy assessment measures was discouraging in this regard, because we found no measure of Somali literacy. Furthermore, almost all the measures we found either assumed that the learners being tested already had basic decoding skills or were age-inappropriate for our population. None could differentiate among the different lowest levels of alphabetic literacy in Somali. In the end, we selected, and adapted for our own use, the Native Language Literacy Screening Device (NLLSD). The Office of Workforce Preparation and Continuing Education in the New York State Education Department expresses its confidence in the measure as a 'means of assessment that...[assists] practitioners in appropriately placing adult learners in ESOL programs and designing instructional strategies appropriate to their skill levels' (Native Language Literacy Screening Device, n.d.: 4). This tool, available in twenty-seven languages (but not Somali), was suited to our limitations in that it can be administered by individuals who do not read or write the native language of the student. The assessment is based on observation of the learner's behavior while taking the test. It is not a comprehensive literacy test. The instructions are written in the native language, and the administrator asks individuals to complete the test on their own, watching them to get a very general sense of their relative comfort in performing the reading and writing tasks. An English language version was also administered. The measures ask participants to write basic personal information (for example, name, address, and phone number) and answer simple questions (for example, Where were you born? In what year did you come to the United States?). This is followed by a number of short personal narratives that the participant reads silently. Finally, the participant is asked to write a similar short narrative.

We adapted the NLLSD for use in our study. First, we created a Somali version[12] of the test, based on the English-language version provided. We asked our participants to do the Somali literacy test first, and later the English literacy test. In each administration of an NLLSD version, the researcher watched the participant for evidence of relative ease or effort in reading and writing, and took detailed notes about such behaviors as tracing the printed lines with a finger, sub-vocalization, fluency if reading aloud, and speed in task performance. We developed an analytic rubric for use in ranking the participants' observed behaviors and writing samples on a scale from 1 to 9. This rubric, presented in Appendix A, operationalizes fluency and comfort level in the very early levels of reading and writing the alphabetic scripts of both English and their native language, Somali.

The researchers conferred and agreed on all their ratings using these rubrics by comparing their observational notes and by examining the writing samples together. L1 and L2 literacy test results were calculated separately using the rubric; then the two scores were added and a mean literacy score was calculated to place participants into one of two overall literacy groups. The rationale for use of a mean score rather than separate scores for L1 and L2 alphabetic literacy is that Cummins's interdependence hypothesis (1979, 1981) suggests that literacy skills, once acquired, generalize quite easily across languages. If Olson (2002) is right that it is alphabetic print literacy that enables one to think in terms such as 'word', and if Cummins is right that literacy skills apply across languages, then we reasoned that it is likely that the process Olson describes would also apply across languages.

Participants with mean alphabetic literacy level scores between 1 and 6 became members of a low-literacy group, and participants with mean alphabetic literacy level scores from 8 to 9 constituted a moderate-literacy group. We use the term 'moderate' literacy to describe this group rather than 'high' intentionally. None of our participants could be described as having 'high' alphabetic literacy levels. Indeed, none appeared to have a literacy level that was commensurate with his or her grade in school. We have guessed that an average child in the upper primary grades could have attained our top literacy level score of 9. Certainly, the alphabetic literacy levels of all the adolescent and adult participants in this study fell far below what is normally assumed for comparably aged participants in other published SLA studies.

Assessing oral English proficiency of participants

The speech production of all our participants appeared to us to be strikingly fluent and colloquial, and our interactions contained very few breakdowns in communication. The participants demonstrated strong pragmatic skills in their use of oral English, routinely initiating small talk with the adult researchers before and after doing the tasks and consistently back-channeling throughout the conversation (that is, 'oh', 'yeah', 'mhm'). However, we needed an objective, independent measure of our participants' general oral proficiency levels in English. To obtain this, we asked two experienced SPEAK test (Speaking Proficiency English Assessment Kit 1982) raters to score each participant's oral language proficiency on a scale of 10–60, by using the SPEAK rating criteria to rate narrative speech samples from the audiotaped data-set. While administering the entire SPEAK test would have taken more time than we felt we could ask of our thirty-five participants, we decided that we could use the scale to rate participants' oral proficiency, given that the samples were rated by trained raters, following Swierzbin's procedure (2004).

Participant group assignments for the three analyses

The three analyses of the data are the recast analysis appearing in Chapter 4, the elicited-imitation analysis in Chapter 5, and the narrative analysis in Chapter 6. We gathered alphabetic literacy and oral proficiency data using the procedures described above, from thirty-five participants, all adolescent or adult Somali immigrants living in Minnesota. Based on their scores on the literacy measure, as described above, we selected from among our original thirty-five participants two subsets of participants for further study, one consisting of those with the lowest literacy level scores in the larger group, and the other of those with the highest literacy level scores.

The eight participants chosen ranged in age from 15 to 27 and reported having been in the United States for between three and seven years. As is typical of Somali refugees of their age group, they had experienced interrupted schooling and many years in refugee camps before arriving in the USA. For this reason, even the four participants in Table 3.2 who scored the highest on our literacy measures were still not alphabetically literate at the level of peers of comparable age with uninterrupted schooling. By the same token, the four participants scoring the lowest in literacy were not entirely illiterate in an alphabetic script, having all attended US schools and been exposed to print. Indeed, most of the participants reported studying the Quran or otherwise engaging with print in out-of-school activities.

The participants in the two literacy groups reported different levels of support for alphabetic literacy in their lives. The four in the moderate-literacy group all reported having literate and educated adults in their lives who had taught them how to read and write in Somali, which, like English, uses an alphabetic script. They also reported that they tried to find reading materials in Somali, such as the local Somali newspaper and books in Somali available at the public library. One participant said that she had tried to teach her friends how to read and write in Somali. These participants performed the simple English and Somali literacy tasks in the NLLSD with relative confidence and ease.

In contrast, the four participants with the lowest scores on the NLLSD reported no support for Somali literacy in their backgrounds, nor did they report having any print materials, either Somali or English, in their homes. All but one could decode at least some written text on the NLLSD, but their attempts to read in English and Somali demonstrated a lack of fluency and the use of strategies to aid in their processing of the text, such as pointing at and reading words one by one, sounding words out, and using much subvocalization (or sounding-out of words) to comprehend the text. Three of the four participants in this group did not attempt to write in Somali on the test at all. Nevertheless, it seemed that all the participants had some basic notions of text in English and/or Somali, such as knowledge that text carries meaning, that letters have sounds that make words, that there are word boundaries, and so on.

Like Philp (2003), we assessed the developmental stage of our eight participants in terms of whether they produced non-formulaic interrogatives of any given developmental stage in at least two different contexts. Using this criterion, all the participants were determined to be at stage 5. They produced between 6 and 28 spontaneous and accurate stage 5 questions as they worked through the task protocol, described below.

Table 3.2 shows that the low-literacy group had mean scores on the literacy measure ranging from 3.5 to 6, while the moderate-literacy group had mean scores ranging from 8 to 9. The eight participants who took part in recast and narrative analyses are shown in Table 3.2. As seen in Table 3.2, years of schooling and alphabetic print literacy level do not coincide at all for these individuals; reported years of schooling is an unreliable measure of actual literacy level. These descriptive data illustrate why it is not adequate in studies with low-literate learners to estimate their alphabetic literacy levels based on their reported years of schooling: a procedure that is, unfortunately, commonly used even in otherwise rigorous studies in cognitive psychology. A year of schooling does not necessarily mean a year of reading instruction. For example, a year of schooling in a refugee camp could easily have involved irregular meetings with peer tutors, reliance on oral recitation, and little actual reading instruction. In Table 3.2, four participants who all reported having three years of schooling in the USA have very different measured alphabetic literacy levels: Ubax and Fawzia are in the low-literacy group (with mean literacy levels of 3.5 and 6 respectively), and Faadumo and Sufia are in the moderate-literacy group (with literacy levels of 9 and 8).

Table 3.2 shows that the two alphabetic literacy groups are similar, but not identical, to one another in terms of age, gender, literacy level, years in the USA, years of schooling, and oral proficiency rating in English. We also recognize that this study has very few participants, and so variation among the participants cannot be ignored. We are not able to present the multiple ways important factors such as past experiences with alphabetic print literacy, gender, and trauma may have played a role in the participants' performance. Furthermore, we know we have deeply ingrained assumptions about what constitutes alphabetic print literacy. We are still uncovering what we assume and do not know about alphabetic literacy and orality across cultures.

It was important to establish alphabetic literacy level, oral language proficiency level, and stage of acquisition of the two groups we wished to compare to confirm that the groups were as similar as possible, given the caveats above. The dependent variables we were interested in related to our participants' oral language processing of grammatical structures in English (that is, question formation, and morphological marking in narrative tasks). These tasks, and the data collection procedure, will now be described.

Participant	Age	Gender	Literacy level				Years in USA	Years schooling		Oral proficiency SPEAK rating
			Group	Literacy mean	L1	L2		Pre-USA	USA	
Abukar	15	M	Low	5	4	6	4.5	0	4.5	50
Najma	27	F	Low	5.5	5	6	3	7	1.5	40
Ubax	17	F	Low	3.5	0	7	3	0	3	40
Fawzia	20	F	Low	6	6	6	3	0	3	30
Khalid	16	M	Moderate	8.5	8.5	8.5	7	0	7	50
Faadumo	18	F	Moderate	9	9	9	3	0	3	40
Moxammed	17	M	Moderate	9	9	9	7	0	7	40
Sufia	15	F	Moderate	8	9	7	3	0	3	30

Notes

[1] The recast analysis is described in Chapter 4 and the narrative analysis in Chapter 6.

[2] Names are pseudonyms.

Table 3.2 Participant profile for recast and narrative analyses

Data collection

Data were collected for all three analyses in the course of one or two individual sessions carried out individually, always with the same researcher. Each participant met a researcher individually in a quiet non-school setting such as an empty homework-help center, or a library study room. Each session followed the same six data-elicitation procedures, using the instruments and procedures described below:

1 introductory conversation to put participant at ease;
2 two spot-the-difference tasks;
3 three story-completion tasks;
4 three story-retell tasks in narration;
5 two elicited-imitation tasks; and
6 literacy measure (L1 after first session; L2 after second session).

The interactive tasks Philp (2003) used, as well as those we created, were piloted with adult English-language learners. The piloting phase led to the decision not to use Philp's picture-drawing task because we decided the task of drawing would interfere too much with the oral interaction, and because we learned that the Somali youth we were likely to recruit would probably find drawing either difficult because of lack of experience in this mode or religiously unacceptable. The literacy measures were piloted with adult English-language learners with limited formal schooling. The elicited-imitation tasks were not piloted.

Procedure for data collection

Each session began with small talk and some questions about past and present schooling experiences. We also asked participants if we could record the session. Participants were asked when they had come to the United States and what other languages they spoke. Participants told us about their schools, their teachers, their classes, and their friends. It was common for them to report many years spent in refugee camps and multiple moves before settling in their current place of residence in the United States.

Some of the subsequent tasks we asked the participants to do were designed (in a partial replication of Philp 2003) to elicit questions from the participants; these constituted the 'recast tasks'. When the participant made grammatical errors in these elicited questions, the researcher provided recasts (implicit corrections) and signaled the participant to repeat the recast. We began the task protocol by telling participants about the tasks and telling them that while they were doing the tasks, we might correct some of the things they said. We explained that when we wanted to correct them we would stop briefly and knock twice on the table. We would say the correction and then ask them to repeat what we said as precisely as possible. This part of the procedure was used in Philp's study. She bases her argument for why an auditory cue to recall was better than a verbal cue on Baddeley (1990), who showed that an irrelevant verbal cue given before participants were asked to recall something impeded performance while a non-speech sound used to cue recall did not disrupt performance. After giving the recast and eliciting the recall from the participant, we would answer the question asked. In our study, the knocking cue typically became unnecessary as students became accustomed to the procedure. In other words, when we stopped and offered a recast of the incorrect trigger utterance, the participant typically attempted recall without any additional verbal or non-verbal cues.

The NLLSD native-language literacy measure (in Somali) was completed only after the participant had finished the first round of tasks. This sequencing was deliberate; we wanted to avoid creating an academic test-like atmosphere and felt that the informal conversation and more participatory tasks would relax the participant, be more respectful, and aid in developing a more communicative or collaborative relationship. Participants then either returned for a second session or took a break before beginning the second session. This second session consisted of the same sequence of tasks, but with the English-language version of the NLLSD literacy measure at the end instead. While Philp's participants (2003) did the tasks in five meetings, each 20 minutes long, our participants did them in two sessions that totaled from 60 to 150 minutes. Some needed more time to complete the tasks, others were given breaks to pray or eat.

Elicitation tasks

We believed that it was essential for data-collection activities to be similar to the sorts of activities the participants encountered in contexts they were familiar with, such as adult literacy classes or typical ESL classrooms. If our data-collection procedures had this kind of face validity, we felt we would be better able to recruit and retain participants.

1 *Spot-the-difference tasks.* The first type of task participants were asked to do in the protocol was a classic 'spot-the-difference' task. The participant and the researcher each had similar but slightly different pictures and the participant asked the researcher questions to identify minor differences between the two pictures. The purpose of the task was to elicit questions in English. When the question was target-like, the interaction proceeded naturally, with the researcher responding to the question with declarative sentences. When the participant produced incorrect question forms, the researcher knocked twice on the table, recast the question, and then asked the learner to repeat the recast. After this, the researcher replied to the intended meaning of the question and the participant continued.[13] Figure 3.1 provides an example of the kind of spot-the-difference task used.

2 *Story-completion tasks.* Participants also performed story-completion tasks, following the protocol described in Philp (2003). In each of the six story-completion tasks, the researcher presented to the participant a sequence of drawings depicting a story, albeit in a way that begged clari-

Figure 3.1 Spot-the-difference task

fication. The researcher would lay one card at a time on the table, and the participant would ask questions about the drawing to determine what the story was about. The researcher would first recast any incorrect question forms and then answer the question, attempting to make the story interesting. This continued until all the pictures, typically six, were revealed and the story was completed. Figure 3.2 shows a set of pictures we used. The basic plot of this story is that a young man (we will call him Ahmed) got up late because his clock stopped during the night and his alarm did not go off. Then he had to hurry to get ready and had to search for his keys and bus money all over his apartment. Then he missed the city bus and had to try to catch a ride from someone in his neighborhood. Luckily, he saw a friend pull over. But the friend had pulled over to clear the snow from his windshield and had not seen him standing on the street. At the same time the friend got out of the car to clear off the snow, Ahmed got in the car on the passenger's side. When his friend had cleared the snow off the windshield, he was surprised to see Ahmed in the car. The friend gave him a ride to school/work.

3 *Story-retell tasks in narration.* In a departure from Philp's protocol (2003), after the story-completion task was completed, we asked the participant to look at the series of pictures on the table and retell the story as if they were telling it to someone who did not know it. The goal was to elicit a coherent narrative from each participant. However, the task sometimes required prompting, so it was not always a fluent monologue carried out by the participants.

4 *Elicited-imitation tasks.* Finally, participants were asked to complete a set of elicited-imitation (EI) tasks. The researcher asked each participant to repeat after her a series of 28 interrogative utterances. In the 'short' EI task, each sentence was eight syllables long; in the 'long' set, each of the 28 interrogative utterances was fifteen syllables long. Though both long and short questions were elicited, only the short questions were analyzed. This is because the longer questions clearly exceeded the short-term-memory capacity of some of the participants (G. Miller 1956; Baddeley 1995). The following examples come from the short EI task and are matched to Stages 4, 5, and 6 using the stages of acquisition outlined by by Pienemann and colleagues (Pienemann and Johnston 1987; Pienemann, Johnston, and Brindley 1988).

Stage 4 copula in wh-Q: What is the name of the teacher?
Stage 5 inversion wh-Q (no do support): What is the new drug store selling?
Stage 4 copula in yes/no Q: Is she nice to the young children?
Stage 6 embedded Q: Would you ask if I can attend?

In addition, there were three practice utterances at the start of the task and six non-interrogative distractor utterances scattered throughout. Participants were told that they would hear a sentence just once, and that they should immediately repeat it as accurately as possible. If a participant had difficulty

(A)

(B)

(C)

(D)

(E)

(F)

Figure 3.2 Story-completion task

with recall, the researcher waited until the participant indicated that he or she could go no further. A list of the EI sentences used in this study and the question acquisition stage each one targets appears in Appendix B.

Summary

In Chapter 3, we have described our methodological stance, our procedures for participant recruitment, and the characteristics of our participants. We also described all the instrumentation we used to elicit data (that is, tests, tasks, and their respective protocols), providing examples of the stimulus materials we used. In each of the chapters that follow we begin with the research questions for one of the three parts of our study, and then describe the way we analyzed the data in order to answer each set of research questions. Each chapter compares characteristics of the oral production of English by our two alphabetic literacy groups. Part One of our study, reported in Chapter 4, examines the accuracy of participants' recall of recasts of their English L2 questions. Part Two, in Chapter 5, deals with the participants' repetition of English L2 questions in elicited-imitation versus recast tasks. Part Three, in Chapter 6, describes grammatical features of English used by the two alphabetic literacy groups in oral narration. We begin in Chapter 4 with the recast study, a partial replication of Philp (2003).

Notes

1 See http://www.westbankcc.org/ for neighborhood information.
2 See http://www.ci.minneapolis.mn.us/neighborhoods/cedarriverside_profile_home.asp for a neighborhood description.
3 See http://en.wikipedia.org/wiki/Cedar-Riverside%2C_Minneapolis for information about the neighborhood.
4 Somalia has not had a central government since the fall of the Siad Barre regime in 1991, which resulted in significant population shifts. Some of the reasons for the collapse of this government and Somalia's challenges to re-establish itself can be traced back to colonial and pre-colonial days. Somalia's European colonial period began in 1884 at the Berlin Conference (Kongokonferenz), where Somalia, along with many other African countries, was partitioned among and between European and neighboring countries, principally Ethiopia, with which Somalia has had many conflicts. 'To this day, Muslim militants, with support from nationalist and clan elements, continue to wage a holy-cum-nationalist war against the occupying Ethiopian forces and those of the Transitional Federal Government' (Abukar Ali, May 25, 2008, personal communication).
5 The people of Somalia are often thought to be of one ethnicity and culturally fairly homogeneous. There are, however, other ethnicities (e.g. the Somali Bantu). In addition to the Bantus, there are three Somali clans considered to be of low caste and treated as outcasts. They are the Yibir, the

Midgan, and the Tumal. They face restrictions, prejudice, discrimination, harassment, and attacks in East Africa as well as in the Diaspora (Fangen 2006).

6 The size of the population is difficult to calculate because it changes dramatically every year due to different refugee policies and fluctuations in migration from other states to and from Minnesota. Furthermore, official census figures are often inaccurate, because families living in rental properties are likely to report the number of residents allowed on the lease, not the actual number living in the dwelling. See http://www.macalester.edu/anthropology/ref_imm/somali_main.html for more demographic information about Somalis in Minnesota.

7 These estimates were published by the Minnesota Office of Geographic and Demographic Analysis and are derived from new enrollment data from the Department of Education, data from the Minnesota Department of Health's Office of Refugee Health and Vital Statistics, the US Department of Homeland Security's Immigration Statistics, and the 2000 Census. Retrieved on March 20, 2008, from http://www.mnplan.state.mn.us/resource.html?Id=7193

8 See http://factfinder.census.gov for state demographic data.

9 See http://www.bbc.co.uk/london/content/articles/2004/08/11/communities_somali_feature.shtml for more information about Somalis in London.

10 See http://webhome.idirect.com/~siao/background.html for more information about Somalis in Toronto.

11 The term 'consent' is reserved for individuals who are 8 or older and the term 'assent' is used when minors agree to participate in a study. We were required to obtain consent from parents of minors as well.

12 Literacy in the Somali language is a relatively recent phenomenon. In 1972 Siad Barre's government determined that Somali would be written using the Roman script (Warsame 2001). This monumental event was accompanied by a massive literacy campaign. It is claimed that basic literacy went from 5% to over 50% for Somalis over 15 years of age (UNICEF n.d.). However, as of September 2008, Somalia has a literacy rate of about 37.8% (49.7% male; 25.8% female). See https://www.cia.gov/library/publications/the-world-factbook/geos/so.html#People. 'Lack of education represents one of the country's biggest challenges as it tries to rebuild with a generation of youth who can barely read or write' (Sanders 2007).

13 Three spot-the-difference tasks and three story-completion tasks were exactly the same tasks used in Philp (2003). We created four additional tasks based on these models. The original picture tasks were developed at the Language Acquisition Research Centre (LARC) with funding from Language Australia.

4
Noticing recasts: corrective oral feedback on L2 forms

Many recent studies have focused on the way corrective feedback is supposed to trigger 'noticing': a process where the L2 learner's attention is attracted to the form that received the corrective feedback. The feedback may engage the process of cognitive comparison on the part of the L2 learner, because it causes the learner, in real time, to compare his or her utterance with an alternate target-like utterance. But, as we have pointed out, all these studies have been restricted to a population of literate L2 learners. Does the alphabetic print literacy level of adult L2 learners affect the degree to which they notice oral recasts on L2 form? In this chapter we consider the relationship between Somali English-language learners' degree of alphabetic print literacy and the accuracy with which they repeat oral recasts of their erroneous question forms.

While 'noticing', as we point out in Chapter 2, cannot be directly observed, we assume in our study on recasts that we may infer that noticing has taken place when the learner modifies production (resulting in 'uptake') following corrective feedback, as in:

ABUKAR	Ok, Where, they?	(Ungrammatical trigger)
RESEARCHER	Where are they?	(Correction: recast)
ABUKAR	Where are they?	(Accurate recall/uptake)

In this example, Abukar presumably noticed the correction in the recast, since he was able to repeat it accurately. This uptake may be temporary, restricted to short-term memory, or may, in fact, lead to acquisition.

As we saw in Chapter 2, SLA research has focused on literate learners (mostly adults) but not on learners who are not literate in any alphabetic script. Such low-literate L2 learners may lack the cognitive and metalinguistic tools needed to make the best use of recasts. The study described in this chapter aims to initiate research on the impact of alphabetic print literacy on oral processing of corrective feedback in SLA.

Recast study on 'noticing'

As explained in Chapter 3, we chose to partially replicate Philp (2003). Philp focused her analysis on learners' 'noticing' of recasts, where 'noticing' is operationalized as learners' accurate recall of recasts of their errors. One of the reasons we chose Philp's study for partial replication was because it was one of few we could find that explored the issue of noticing entirely in the oral modes, using procedures that did not require the participants to be literate.

Philp (2003) provided recasts on question formation to thirty-three college-age, highly-educated L2 learners of six different L1s. The participants were divided into high, intermediate, and low groups according to their stage of acquisition of question formation (Pienemann and Johnson 1987). Philp's results showed that, on average, recall of these recasts was accurate 60–70 percent of the time across the three groups. When the learners' level of acquisition of question forms matched the level of forms provided in the recasts on questions, at least 70 percent of the recalls were accurate, with 90 percent showing some modification from the erroneous 'trigger' utterance. Philp concluded the learners' accuracy in repeating the recasts was affected by their processing biases and readiness to learn the target structure, the length of the recast, and the number of changes the recast made to the learner's initial non-target question. Citing Baddeley (1986), Cowan (1995), and N. Ellis (1996), Philp concluded that increasing the length of the recasts to more than five morphemes, or making two, three, or more changes in the recast, pushed the limits of the learners' working memory.

As explained in Chapter 3, in our partial replication we posed research questions and hypotheses similar to those in Philp (2003), but we added the construct of alphabetic literacy level to the constructs of learner level and stage of question acquisition she explored. We formulated three general research questions to guide our quantitative analysis of the performance of the eight low-literate learners:

1 Is the accuracy of recall[1] of a recast related to the alphabetic literacy level of the learner?
2 Is the accuracy of recall of a recast related to the length of the recast? Do learners at higher alphabetic literacy levels do better?
3 Is the accuracy of recall of a recast related to the number of changes made by the recast? Do learners at higher alphabetic literacy levels do better?

In addition, we provide a detailed qualitative analysis of the performance of one of these low-literate participants.[2]

Recast study: quantitative analysis

The eight participants

The participants in the recast study were described in detail in Table 3.2. From the initial pool of thirty-five Somali participants from whom we gathered data, we selected eight for inclusion in the recast study: four whose scores on the English and Somali alphabetic literacy measures were among the highest in the group of thirty-five, and four whose literacy scores were among the lowest.

Data collection and analysis

The two tasks that were analyzed as part of the recast study, described in Chapter 3, were spot-the-difference tasks and story-completion tasks; both elicited questions from the participants. The oral interactions between the participants and researchers in completing the spot-the-difference and story-completion tasks were tape-recorded and transcribed. All questions asked by the participants, both correct and incorrect, were identified and analyzed.

To analyze the participants' oral questions, we followed Philp in adopting the framework outlined by Pienemann et al. (1988), which predicts six stages in the acquisition of English question forms. Participants' non-target questions (triggers), researcher recasts of the triggers, and the participant recalls of the recasts were transcribed and coded. We followed Philp's coding procedure and categorized (*a*) the length of each recast; (*b*) the number and type of corrections in each recast; (*c*) the degree of accuracy of the participants' recall of these recasts; and (*d*) the question stages occurring in both the trigger and the recast. The interrater agreement rate in performing these categorizations was 99.5 percent.

Recast length was operationalized, following Philp (2003), in terms of number of morphemes, with a recast consisting of six or more morphemes classified as 'long', and a recast of five or fewer morphemes as 'short'.[3] The number of changes to the trigger that appeared in the recast was also calculated according to Philp's procedures (1999, 2003).[4] The degree of accuracy of the participants' recall was categorized as correct, modified, or no recall, following Philp (2003). A response was judged *correct* when the recall of the question form exactly matched that of the recast, as in the following:

(1) Trigger   What she doing?
    Recast   What is she doing? *two knocks*
    Recall   What is she doing? (correct)

The response was judged as *modified* if only some of the changes modeled in the recast were made, as in the following:

(2) Trigger   He is surprised?
    Recast   Is he surprised? *two knocks*
    Recall   Is he is surprised? (modified)

If none of the target changes was recalled, the response was judged *no recall*, as in the following:

(3) Trigger   What color it is?
    Recast   What color is it? *two knocks*
    Recall   What colorrrrr (no recall)

The independent variable was alphabetic print literacy level and the dependent variables were (*a*) proportion of correct recall; (*b*) recast length; and (*c*) number of changes in recast. Because of our small sample size, we made minor modifications to some categories. In addition to Philp's category of proportion of correct recall, we set up another category called proportion of *correct and modified* recall, in order to capture all instances of uptake, even when uptake was not 100 percent accurate.[5] In order to get large enough counts for recasts with more than one change, the counts for two changes and three or more (3+) changes were combined into a single category of two or more (2+) changes.

Examples of the 'number-of-changes' dependent variable are provided below.

Recalling recasts with 1 change:

(4) Trigger   Why he's so happy?
    Recast   Why is he so happy? *two knocks*
    Recall   Why is he so happy? (correct)

Recalling recasts with 2+ changes:

(5) Trigger   What he doing, the man in the sitting chair?
    Recast   What is the man sitting in the chair doing? *two knocks*
    Recall   What is the man sitting in the chair doing? (correct)

Statistical measure: exact permutation analysis

Parametric statistical analyses, which are standard in applied linguistics, require the use of larger sample sizes in order to meet their mathematical assumptions of normally distributed variables. However, the sample size we have in this study is too small for us to make this assumption. Fortunately, in recent years, statisticians have developed new non-parametric methods that can be used to establish statistical significance of difference between groups when working with small, non-normally distributed samples of the sort we have in this study. In our quantitative analysis, we used exact permutation analysis, a resampling method that is ideal for small sample sizes such as ours because it does not assume an underlying distribution for the test statistic (Efron and Tibshirani 1993; Good 2001; Chernick 2007). To our knowledge, applied linguists have not yet used exact permutation analysis in analyzing their data, even though this method is now in wide use in other fields (particularly biostatistics). Detailed information on exact permutation analysis as a statistical measure is provided in Efron and Tibshirani (1993), Good (2001), and Bigelow et al. (2006).

Results

Research question one

Is the accuracy of recall of a recast related to the alphabetic literacy level of the learner?

Recast type	Mean literacy level		p-value
	Low (1–6)	Moderate (8–9)	
Correct recall			
All	0.633	0.779	0.057
Long	0.676	0.751	0.214
Short	0.657	0.844	0.086
1 change	0.533	0.597	0.243
2+ changes	0.429	0.723	0.143
Correct and modified recall			
All	0.852	0.928	0.043
Long	0.827	0.907	0.086
Short	0.851	0.974	0.071
1 change	0.849	0.909	0.114
2+ changes	0.820	1.000	0.014

Notes
[1] The possible score range on literacy level is 1–9.
[2] All p-values are one-tailed.

Table 4.1 Relationships among literacy level, recast length and complexity, and recall (correct versus modified and correct)

To address this question, two separate analyses were conducted, one for each dependent measure: proportion of correct recall, and proportion of correct and modified recall.

In all tests on both dependent measures, the mean scores of the moderate-literacy group are higher than those of the low-literacy group (Table 4.1). The impact of alphabetic literacy level on recall using the first criterion (the mean proportion of *correct* recalls) was in the expected direction, approaching but not reaching significance at $p < 0.05$ for several tests according to recast type. However, use of the second criterion (mean proportion of correct *and modified* recall) produced much lower p-values, two of which reached significance at the $p < 0.05$ level. The moderate-literacy group recalled, in correct or modified form, all recasts significantly more often than the less literate group ($p = 0.043$), and also recalled correct and modified recasts with 2+ changes significantly more often than the less literate group ($p = 0.014$). We conclude that alphabetic print literacy level is significantly related to the accuracy of recall of recasts.

Research question two

Is the accuracy of recall of a recast related to the length of the recast? Do learners at higher alphabetic literacy levels do better?

To address this question, we used several measures. We subtracted the proportion of recall (correct, or correct and modified) for short recasts from the proportion of recall for long recasts. A one-tailed p-value of $p = 0.344$

suggested that, for the group as a whole, the participants' *proportion of correct recall* was not dependent on the length of the recast. We also measured the difference between long and short recasts for the group as a whole based on *proportion of correct and modified recall*; an exact permutation test of the mean difference score resulted in a one-tailed *p*-value of $p = 0.133$. There is no statistical evidence that, for the group as a whole, the participants' *proportion of correct and modified recall* was dependent on the length of the recast. Additional analyses were conducted to see if the participants' mean alphabetic literacy levels interacted with recast length. Differences between the two mean literacy level groups with respect to the length of the recasts they received were tested via permutation tests. Table 4.2 indicates that there were no statistically significant differences in recast length between the two alphabetic literacy level groups. The mean difference in *proportion of correct recall of long and short recasts* between the high and low mean literacy groups is presented in Table 4.3. The *p*-value suggests there is no evidence of a difference between recalling short and long recasts for the different mean alphabetic literacy groups.

To sum up: although we tested the possibility using different measures, there was no evidence that these learners' ability to recall a recast was related to the length of the recast. This finding is strikingly different from that of Philp (2003) with regard to recast length.

Research question three

Is the accuracy of recall of a recast related to the number of changes made by the recast? Do learners at higher alphabetic literacy levels do better?

To explore this question, we analyzed the data in several ways. We asked first whether there is a difference in the dependent measures for the group as a whole between recasts with 1 change and recasts with 2+ changes. The *proportion of correct recall for recasts with 1 change* was subtracted from the *proportion of correct recall for recasts with 2+ changes* to form the dependent measure. An exact permutation test produced a one-tailed

Recast type	Mean literacy level		*p*-value
	Low (1–6)	Moderate (8–9)	
All	5.46	6.13	0.229
Long	6.73	7.25	0.329
Short	4.46	4.17	0.600

Notes
[1] The possible score range on literacy level is 1–9.
[2] All p-values are two-tailed.

Table 4.2 Mean morpheme length of recasts by literacy level

Type of difference	Mean literacy level		p-value
	Low (1–6)	Moderate (8–9)	
Correct recall			
Long–short	0.019	−0.094	0.343
2+ changes–1 change	−0.104	0.126	0.186
Correct and modified recall			
Long–short	−0.025	−0.068	0.329
2+ changes–1 change	−0.029	0.91	0.171

Notes
[1] The possible score range on literacy level is 1–9.
[2] All p-values are one-tailed.

Table 4.3 Mean difference in proportion of recalled recasts by literacy level

p-value of *p* = 0.449. So there is no statistical evidence that, as a group, the participants' accuracy of recall was dependent on the number of changes in the recast. Then we tested the difference for the group as a whole between recasts with 1 and 2+ changes based on the *proportion of combined correct and modified recalls* and found no statistical evidence that the participants' recall was related to the number of changes in the recast.

Another way of answering Research Question Three is to determine whether, *within* our participant group, the number of changes in the recast had a significantly different impact on the moderately literate versus less literate groups. We measured this difference first in *proportion of correct recall*, and second in *proportion of correct and modified recall* combined. Using the criterion of *correct* recall, we see in Table 4.3 the difference between proportion of correct recall of recasts with 1 change versus 2+ changes for the moderate and low alphabetic literacy levels. The *p*-values present no statistical evidence of a difference using this criterion. Next we asked the same question using the criterion of *correct and modified* recall. Table 4.1 presents the proportion of correct and modified recalls, by learners in the moderate and low alphabetic literacy groups, of recasts with only 1 change and recasts with 2+ changes. The difference between the two literacy groups for recasts with two or more changes (*p* = 0.014) is significant. This suggests that the moderate alphabetic literacy group recalled correctly or in modified form a larger proportion of recasts with 2+ changes when compared to the lower literacy group. The difference between the two literacy groups for recasts with just 1 change was not statistically significant (but in the expected direction, moderate > low). Table 4.3 presents the *difference* between proportion of correct or modified recalls by the higher and lower mean alphabetic literacy groups of recasts with 1 and 2+ changes. However, the *p*-value suggests that there is no evidence of a different trend between the higher and lower alphabetic literacy groups in differentially recalling, either correctly or in modified form, recasts on the basis of the number of changes.

These findings are complicated. If we consider the difference in mean recall for 1 change and for 2+ changes between the two groups in Table 4.2, we see the difference between the two groups is greater when the recast has more than 2+ changes. The low alphabetic literacy group has a lower average for 2+ changes compared to 1 change, whereas the moderate-literacy group has the opposite trend (higher average recall for 2+ changes). In other words, the two groups went in opposite directions in their responses to recasts containing 1 change versus 2+ changes. This pattern results in a larger difference between groups for 2+ changes, and that difference is statistically significant.

To sum up, there is some statistical evidence to suggest that learners at moderate alphabetic literacy levels performed significantly better than low-literate learners on one of our two measures. When they had to recall recasts that contained 2+ changes, the participants in the moderate alphabetic literacy group performed better than the low-literacy group.

Discussion of quantitative analysis

The quantitative analysis confirms that alphabetic print literacy level was related to the learners' accuracy of recall of oral recasts of their errors in production of interrogatives. The moderately literate group recalled, in correct or modified form, all recasts significantly better than the less literate group. These results suggest that alphabetic literacy affects an L2 learner's cognitive processing of the oral L2. This interpretation is consistent with the evidence presented in Chapter 1 that the decoding skills provided by alphabetic literacy have an impact on the oral processing of adults' native language. This study establishes for the first time that this impact is not limited to oral L1 processing, but also extends to oral L2 processing.

The results of our recast analysis differ in interesting ways from Philp's results (2003) for more-educated and literate participants. Stage of acquisition and proficiency level were controlled in our study, and so could not have caused the significant differences we found. In contrast to Philp (2003), the length of the recast was not a factor for our participants. What could have caused this difference? The most interesting explanation would be that our participants used different cognitive processes than Philp's participants did. Possibly they used semantic processing strategies that were not affected by length (as measured by morpheme count) in the way that metalinguistic processing strategies might be. Length may be a more important factor for alphabetically literate learners who rely more on visual morphosyntactic strategies to process oral language. In Somali culture, as in other traditionally oral cultures, there is a premium placed on memorizing and reciting very long oral narratives in the native language. We also know from the research reviewed in Chapter 1 that alphabetic literacy does not affect an individual's ability to focus on rhyme and rhythm in language form, or to process language semantically. It is theoretically possible that low alphabetic literate individuals like our participants can use non-visual strategies based on their experience memorizing long oral narratives, strategies that capitalize on rhyme, rhythm, or semantic cues to hold more oral language in working memory.

However, there are other possible explanations for the lack of statistical significance of length of recast as a factor for our participants. These must be ruled out before we can confirm the interesting possibility above. For one, our use of correct and modified learner responses, as opposed to Philp's use of only correct responses, could have caused this difference; further research is needed to determine this. For another, it is interesting that some participants had difficulty even with very short recasts, such as the following; such difficulties could have made it difficult to show any statistical trend with increasing length of recasts:

Trigger   *Where he is?
Recast   Where is he?
Recall   *Where he is?

It is impossible without more data to tease apart these factors and say why length of recast had so little impact on recall accuracy in our study.

We found a complicated relationship among alphabetic literacy level, number of changes made by the recast, and participants' accuracy in uptake. While the number of changes in the recast was not significantly related to accuracy of recall for the Somali learners as a group, within the Somali participant pool, the moderate-literacy group produced more correct or modified recalls for recasts with 2+ changes than the less literate group did.

To sum up, the quantitative recast analysis, overall, found that alphabetic literacy level was significantly related to the accuracy of recall of oral recasts of the learners' non-target L2 questions. Less literate learners did not recall oral recasts on question forms as accurately as moderately literate learners. A deeper qualitative analysis of a single participant provides helpful insights into some reasons for these results.

Recast study: qualitative analysis

In the follow-up qualitative analysis of the data, we looked at one participant's interactions in more detail in order to consider the cognitive processes that might be assumed to underlie our participants' performance in recast tasks. We will call this participant Abukar. In documenting in detail the successes and failures of Abukar, a low-literate adolescent, as he tried to process recasts and produce target-like reformulations, we address questions such as these:

- Did he have more difficulty recalling recasts requiring metalinguistic knowledge than recasts requiring semantic knowledge?
- If so, what sorts of metalinguistic knowledge did he seem to lack?

In the following section, we examine in detail the transcripts of his interactions with the researcher in performing the oral tasks we gave him.

Learner background

At the time of the study, Abukar was 15 years old, and in his first year of secondary school at a large urban school in Minneapolis. He was typical of the Somali immigrant adolescents in our study in that during the years when he should have been in school he was experiencing the disruptions of the Somali civil war and subsequent time in refugee camps. Abukar told us he was in a refugee camp for four years, and then came to the United States, at which point he began his formal education. At the time of the study, he had been in the United States, and in school, for four and a half years. The population of his current school was almost entirely African American and Somali. Like the other participants in our quantitative study, Abukar was at stage five in English question development: he had spontaneously produced more than six accurate questions at stage five (that is, questions with subject–auxiliary inversion). His oral proficiency in English was very good; blind raters gave him a SPEAK test score of 50. Outside school, Abukar reported studying the Quran daily and learning words in Arabic and Oromo. He said he spoke both English and Somali every day in and out of school. His English seemed to reflect the urban vernacular he was exposed to, and his dress had a hip-hop aesthetic common among adolescents in this metropolitan area.

Abukar's performance on the tasks

It took Abukar some effort to do the English portion of the alphabetic literacy test. In completing the reading section of the test, he sub-vocalized in order to comprehend the text. He also had trouble with the writing section of the English test. The following is what he wrote on the English literacy test in response to the prompt: 'Tell us why you want to learn English or anything else you would like to tell us.'

> I like play sports, like differen sport basketball, baseball, football.
> I like to learn, my farati [favorite] subject is math gym and reading.

While this writing sample is very minimal, it is entirely comprehensible with impressively accurate spelling. The raters, using the rubric in Appendix A that was developed for the study, assessed Abukar's English alphabetic literacy level as 6 (out of 9).

The Somali literacy test, however, was markedly harder for Abukar than the English test. He decoded the Somali texts very slowly, and again with much sub-vocalization. On the Somali literacy test he did not attempt to write anything in Somali when he was given the same instructions as above. The raters assigned him an alphabetic literacy level of 4 in Somali, again using the rubric in Appendix A.

Thus, Abukar had some ability to read and write in both English and Somali. However, his decoding skills were still laborious in both languages, more so in Somali than in English. We assume his decoding skills had not reached a level of automaticity, and still required some considerable conscious attentional resources.

As described previously, Abukar was instructed to ask oral questions about pictures he was shown. The researcher provided recasts of his questions when they were grammatically inaccurate, tapping on the table to signal the corrections. He was told to repeat each recast when signaled to do so.

Results

In performing the spot-the-difference and narrative question tasks in our study, Abukar's errors in question formation most typically involved failure to invert subject and auxiliary in the present progressive or copula, as in (1) and (2), and the use of a bare verb that was unmarked for tense, as in (3):

(1) ABUKAR ...what, what he is looking?
(2) ABUKAR Why he is mad?
(3) ABUKAR ...why he come this room?

When he made these errors, he received recasts from the researcher that offered correct reformulations of his erroneous question forms.[6] Abukar made many errors involving failure either to mark verbs for tense, or to invert subject and auxiliary in questions. On the one hand, he seemed to evidence very little ability to notice corrections highlighted in recasts of the morphosyntactic form of his questions; on the other hand, he was able to modify his production quickly when a recast focused on a lexical item.

Form-focused recasts

There are multiple examples in the transcript of Abukar's apparent failure to modify his output in response to the researcher's repeated recasts of linguistic segments in his non-target questions. While he did spontaneously produce some stage five questions, many of his questions in these tasks did not include auxiliaries or subject–auxiliary inversion. He had special difficulty with accuracy in, and corrective feedback on, questions with present progressive constructions. Early in the session, for example, we find this episode:

(4) 01 ABUKAR   What he sit on, what he SIT on, or whatever?
    02 RESEARCHER What is he sitting on?
    03 ABUKAR   Mhm.
    04 RESEARCHER What is he sitting on? Again. Repeat.

05 ABUKAR	What he sitting on?
06 RESEARCHER	What IS he sitting on?
07 ABUKAR	Oh. What he sitting on?
08 RESEARCHER	What IS he sitting on?
09 ABUKAR	What IS he sitting on?

In line 01, Abukar uses the bare verb 'sit' and in line 02 he receives a recast in present progressive, where he must notice an inserted auxiliary *is* and an inserted –*ing* on the verb. In line 03, he simply backchannels, which suggests that has not noticed the change in form, but rather treats the recast as a semantic confirmation check. Asked explicitly to repeat in line 04, Abukar produces in line 05 a progressive question without an auxiliary; he has inserted the –*ing* but not the 'is'. This change suggests that he is now trying to focus on form rather than meaning, but is more focused on the –*ing* form than the less-salient *is*. Again receiving the recast with the auxiliary in line 06, he again repeats without the auxiliary in line 07. Perhaps he has been able to retain only a part of the recast in short-term memory and has not noticed the insertion of the auxiliary form. Only when the recast is provided for the third time with the inserted auxiliary form stressed does he insert a stressed auxiliary form in a correct question in line 09. This suggests that the use of stress in the recast helped him notice and insert the auxiliary in the correct position.

The sequence in Example (4) above shows us that Abukar focuses first on meaning, on the semantics of the exchange, and then has difficulty shifting to a focus on form. In trying to focus on form, the transcript suggests that he may have difficulty holding the forms in working memory. In Example (4), the correct auxiliary form *is* must be provided repeatedly in four sequential recasts, in line 02, line 04r, line 06, and line 08, and each recall seems to become more explicit. His success in line 09, retaining the stressed auxiliary *is* form in working memory and inserting it correctly, does not seem to result in any transfer to long-term memory, because in Example (5), only three turns later, we see that he produces exactly the same error: a failure to insert an *is* auxiliary with the –*ing* participle in his question:

(5) 01 ABUKAR	What this girl, reading?
02 RESEARCHER	What IS this girl reading?
03 ABUKAR	What is, is this girl reading?

In line 01, Abukar does produce an –*ing* on the present participle, a form that he was earlier able to correct on the first try in line 05 in Example (4). The recasts provided in Example (4) may have had an influence on his noticing and marking of the participle, though not on his use of the auxiliary, which apparently must be stressed in the recast in order for him to notice and repeat it.

Repeated provisions of recasts, with repeated failure of uptake, are common in Abukar's data. It seems that Abukar often *tries* to focus on form in processing the corrective input in this task; he just has trouble perceiving the target of the correction. Here is another example, again with a bare verb and present progressive recast, given halfway through one of the story-completion tasks:

(6) 01 ABUKAR   Oh. What he try to write down?
    02 RESEARCHER   What IS he trying to write down?
    03 ABUKAR   What he's, he's try to write down?
    04 RESEARCHER   What IS he trying
    05 ABUKAR   What he is t, try to, write down?

Even in Example (7), at the very end of the story-completion task, Abukar continues to omit the auxiliary in the present progressive in question formation, and requires repeated recasts of this error before he produces a correct recall.

(7) 01 ABUKAR   What he thinking about, what he thinking?
    02 RESEARCHER   What is he thinking?
    03 ABUKAR   What is he is thinking?
    04 RESEARCHER   What IS he thinking?
    05 ABUKAR   What IS he thinking?

Even here, at the very end of the interaction, after numerous recasts of this same error, Abukar still seems to have difficulty noticing and then recalling the three elements offered in the recast reformulations: the *–ing* on the present participle, the required auxiliary *be,* and then the inversion of that auxiliary with the subject. After numerous recasts, he still does not seem to have this pattern stored in his long-term memory.

Abukar apparently prefers semantic processing in the examples above, and has extended difficulty in noticing inserted linguistic forms and their word order in processing these recasts of his question forms. These preferences and difficulties on the part of Abukar, who has measurably low levels of alphabetic print literacy, can be interpreted as evidence of difficulty using phonological strategies in short-term memory. Certainly, there does not appear to be much change in Abukar's performance over the time span of the oral tasks we gave him; accordingly, we must assume that the feedback he was given also caused no change in his interlanguage grammar.

There are examples in the transcript that provide us with useful insight into what it is that Abukar does seem to notice in the recasts of his question, instead of noticing aux or *–ing* insertion, or subject–auxiliary inversion. In the following exchange, for example, which occurs just a minute after the exchange in (4), he seems to notice stress patterns rather than linguistic segments. Following a recast that stresses a copula that the researcher would like him to move, he alters the stress placement of his original utterance instead of performing a subject–copula inversion.

(8) 01 ABUKAR   Why he is mad? Why [he], he is mad?
    02 RESEARCHER   [yeah]
    03 RESEARCHER   Why IS he mad?
    04 ABUKAR   Why HE is mad? Why

| 05 RESEARCHER | Why IS he mad? |
| 06 ABUKAR | Why IS he mad? Why is, [is he] ... |

In line 01, Abukar produces an uninverted subject–copula question; in line 03 he receives a recast with the subject and verb correctly inverted, with stress on the copula, which is now in second position. In line 04, Abukar produces exactly the same uninverted word order he originally produced, but now he *stresses the word in second position*, which unfortunately is a pronoun, and he retains the uninverted word order. The linguistic form he seems to have noticed is *second-position stress* rather than inverted word order. (Here again, we recall the difficulty that illiterate participants had with oral syllable and word-inversion tasks in studies such as Adrian, Alegría, and Morais 1995, and the ease with which illiterate participants processed prosodic features like rhyme in that same study). In line 05, the researcher provides exactly the same recast again, and this time, in line 06, Abukar successfully inverts subject and verb, retaining second-position stress. But it has required several repetitions of the recast to achieve success in processing word-order changes.

Vocabulary recasts

Another thing that Abukar has no trouble noticing in the recasts is lexical input. Castro-Caldas, Petersson, Reis, Stone-Elander, and Ingvar (1998) found that illiterate participants have better access to semantic and lexical strategies than to phonological strategies. Based on Castro-Caldas et al. (1998), and other cognitive psychologists who have studied oral language processing by illiterate adults, we would predict that Abukar might find it much easier to process recasts that focus on lexis. And, indeed, our examination of his interaction shows that Abukar does produce immediate uptake of lexical recasts, without requiring the multiple repetitions of recasts that are needed to get him to respond when the target is morphosyntax.[7] Abukar's faster uptake from lexical feedback than from morphosyntactic feedback suggests that his low alphabetic literacy level does not affect his processing of semantic or lexical feedback in the same way that it affects his processing of morphosyntactic feedback. In other words, noticing a lexical gap in his initial utterance appears to be easier than noticing a missing auxiliary or an incorrect order of subject and auxiliary.

At one point it becomes clear that Abukar does not know the word 'jar', which he needs in order to ask his question:

(9) 01 ABUKAR	OK (pause) what is barrel, what is, what is the thing in it?
02	What is there? Is it, is there pennies in it?
03 RESEARCHER	Yeah. Um, again. Are pennies in the jar?
04 ABUKAR	Is, are the penny in the jar?
05 RESEARCHER	Yes. And, um,
06 ABUKAR	(whispers) jar

07 RESEARCHER	you know she's a waitress, so she gets tips,
08 ABUKAR	OK
09 RESEARCHER	at the diner,
10 ABUKAR	mhm
11 RESEARCHER	and every day she puts her tips in a jar
12 ABUKAR	oh. (pause) (xxx xxx)
13 RESEARCHER	Here's the jar.
14 ABUKAR	A jar?

In line 01, Abukar uses a communication strategy (see Tarone 1980), producing 'barrel' in approximation to the word he does not know, which is 'jar'. In line 03, the researcher supplies the word 'jar', and in line 04 Abukar immediately recalls the recast 'jar' accurately. Interestingly, he then does more: he repeats the word 'jar' to himself in line 06; in Vygotskyian terms, he engages in private speech, possibly a strategy to rehearse the new term. Such rehearsal has been claimed to help move the new term from short-term memory to long-term memory (e.g. Tarone 2000a; Ohta 2001). It is interesting that we have observed no evidence of this kind of rehearsal in his processing of syntactic recasts. Abukar hears the new term again as the researcher answers his question in line 11, he hesitates in line 12, and receives an explicit recast again in line 13, with uptake in line 14. Twenty-two turns later, as shown below in (12), Abukar spontaneously uses the new term 'jar' in a new question, suggesting that it is now in long-term memory:

(10) ABUKAR   Oh. Oh. Is this jar have, this jar, is this jar full of money?

Abukar processes this lexical recast very successfully, with immediate accurate recall of the recast lexical item, use of it in rehearsal in private speech, and spontaneous production of the term much later in the interaction. His processing of this lexical recast is much more successful than his processing of syntactic recasts of his morphosyntactic question forms.

To sum up: we have seen in Examples (4) through (8) that recasts targeting auxiliary insertion and subject–auxiliary and subject–copula inversion in interrogatives had to be repeated several times before Abukar successfully recalled them. This occurred even when he was clearly and explicitly trying to focus on form. When trying to do this, he seemed better able to focus on stress position than on rearranging linguistic segments. His difficulties seemed restricted to the processing of corrective input on linguistic segmental form rather than corrective input on semantic content or even stress placement.

Discussion: Abukar's noticing of recasts
of non-target questions

The recasts provided in this study were intended to promote Abukar's noticing of his non-target question formations in English. We would argue that the potential of the recasts in our study to promote noticing was bolstered by the fact that the recasts focused on a single form (questions in English) and resulted in a great deal of input on the same forms: an input flood (Sharwood Smith 1993). As in other recast studies, the first use of a recast was often interpreted by participants in our recast study, not as corrective feedback, but as a confirmation check regarding the semantic meaning of the initial utterance, similar to participants in Lyster (1998a, b). However, all the participants went on to receive repeated recasts that focused on the accuracy of the linguistic segments they produced in asking questions. Each recast was highlighted by the researcher's taps on the table top.

And yet, just as our quantitative results show for the rest of the low alphabetic literacy group, Abukar had difficulty noticing the difference between linguistic segments in his own production and those provided in the recast. Even when asked to repeat several times, and when he seemed to be focused explicitly on trying to imitate a linguistic form, Abukar had difficulty repeating linguistic segments, particularly segments that were devoid of semantic content, such as auxiliary and subject–auxiliary inversion. There was also little evidence of learning of these morphosyntactic forms as the interaction itself unfolded; this behavior did not seem to generalize to later instances in the interaction. Abukar made the same errors repeatedly. Even at the end of the interaction, Example (7), he still had problems inserting the auxiliary *is* into his questions. These failures to benefit from recasts on the morphosyntax of his question formation stand in stark contrast with his success in the same interaction in noticing, uptaking, rehearsing, and spontaneously producing both stress patterns and a new lexical item. These results are consistent with claims like those of Reis and Castro-Caldas (1997), documented in Chapter 2, that illiterate and low-literate adults prefer to use semantic and lexical processing strategies rather than phonological or metalinguistic processing strategies.

The model upon which many SLA researchers base their account of L2 learners' cognitive processing of corrective feedback is based on the work of cognitive psychologists such as Levelt (1992) and Baddeley (2007). It is this cognitive model that was appealed to by Reis and Castro-Caldas (1997) in accounting for the superior performance of literate adults to that of illiterate adults (on their oral language-processing tasks). They argued that literate adults had two types of knowledge, semantic and metalinguistic, to use as tools in processing language input, while illiterate adults had to rely primarily on semantic knowledge, as their lack of alphabetic literacy had not afforded them the metalinguistic knowledge they needed as a second tool for analysis. This model is an input-processing model of cognition in which the learner is conceptualized as an independent unit, who parses linguistic input using multiple types of knowledge, both semantic and metalinguistic, as resources.

Socioculturally-oriented L2 researchers in Lantolf (2000b), who use Vykgotsky's framework (1962) for understanding acquisition processes, would surely agree with these cognitive psychologists that metalinguistic knowledge is used as a tool in the process of language acquisition. However, in explaining the performance of participants like Abukar in responding to the recast task, socio-cultural theorists would also surely want to point out that these participants are not just isolated individuals processing language input but rather are partner-ing the researchers, who provide the recasts in a process of co-construction of language that falls within Vygotsky's Zone of Proximal Development (ZPD) of the learner. In other words, the participants' partners in the interactions we describe in our study (the researchers) are trying to provide scaffolding for them to use in building their linguistic knowledge. As they do so, they make assump-tions about the cognitive processing tools these participants use with that scaffolding. But the tool of metalinguistic analysis that the researcher assumes to exist may in fact be either missing or too fragile to function as an effective tool in parsing the language input being provided. Abukar's low alphabetic literacy skills may not afford him sufficient metalinguistic knowledge to use in parsing the input he receives, forcing him to rely primarily on tools of semantic processing. In sociocultural terms, then, it may be the mismatch between the scaffolders' assumptions about what the learner needs in the way of support, and the learner's actual metalinguistic knowledge that underlies the learner's inability to make good use of the scaffolding provided in the recasts.

Summary

Both our quantitative and qualitative research results reveal that interactional feedback in the form of recasts had relatively little impact on the low-literate learners' correct production of targeted linguistic segments. The lower the alphabetic literacy level of the learner, the less likely it was that learners would recall, either correctly or with some modification, the provided recasts. This lack of accurate recall occurred despite the apparent appropriateness of input level, the multiple repetitions of the same corrective feedback in a kind of input flood, and persistent effort on the part of the learners to repair the lin-guistic form of their utterances.

We believe that there are major implications of our findings in this recast study for SLA research on attention and awareness. The ability to attend to and analyze oral L2 input in terms of segmental linguistic units may depend on an individual's prior alphabetic print literacy level. Perhaps it is alphabetic literacy that affords L2 learners the ability to attend to 'surface elements' in the input, to store these in working memory, and to engage in the process of cognitive comparison that is required for L2 acquisition. Low-literate adults and adolescents, essentially unstudied by SLA researchers thus far, do not use the same strategies for oral language processing that literate learners do. Low-literate adults' strategies appear to cause them significant difficulty com-pleting oral tasks that require the noticing and manipulation of linguistic form. Low-literate adults may find it difficult to use morphosyntactic recasts as a way to discover certain kinds of non-target-like forms in their own interlanguages.

We must not forget, however, that the participants in our study have already been successful in acquiring important elements of English, their L2. Some of them have reached relatively high levels of proficiency, as measured by their SPEAK test scores. Although their English interlanguage omits many semantically empty linguistic units and exhibits incorrect word order, they have clearly acquired quite a few L2 forms, using the language-processing strategies they have. For example, they have clearly acquired a functioning systematic interlanguage. Their interlanguage system is solid: indeed, it seems resistant to corrective feedback in certain areas—perhaps even fossilized!

We have seen that some L1 acquisition scholars believe that children must first have alphabetic literacy before they are able to acquire a defined set of more complex syntactic structures that characterize the written language (Ravid and Tolchinsky 2002). In this view, while a set of simple syntactic structures is acquirable without alphabetic print literacy, there is a set of more complex syntactic structures (such as those identified by Biber (1988) and Biber et al. (2002) as characterizing the use of language for literacy) that may not be acquired until after several years of literate experience. One possibility in SLA is that some L2 forms may be easily acquirable without alphabetic literacy, but others may require metalinguistic cognitive comparison using the tool of visuographic representation. Thus, while illiterate or low-literate L2 learners could become quite fluent in the use of a set of simple syntactic structures, and learn to use semantic and lexical strategies in a sophisticated way to achieve pragmatic and sociolinguistic goals, they still might not acquire some of the syntactic structures that are most frequent in written language. Some of the syntactic structures useful for linguistic literacy in the L2 might, in the end, require prior alphabetic print literacy. We will explore this possibility in Chapter 6.[8]

Notes

1 We used the term 'recall' in our research questions and in our first published study because Philps used it. We recognize that 'recall' usually implies retrieval from memory (typically long term) rather than the immediate repetition that actually occurred in both studies, but, in the spirit of partial replication, we use the language of the replicated study.

2 A full description of this qualitative study may be found in Tarone and Bigelow (2007).

3 Morpheme counts were based on guidelines used in a child language development study by Bonnie Johnson at the University of Florida, posted at http://web.clas.ufl.edu/users/bwjohn/4004/Materials/MLU.htm. Each word counts as a morpheme, and suffixes (i.e. plural *–s*, past tense *–ed*, progressive *–ing*, third-person present tense *–s*, possessive *'s*, and contractions) counted as additional morphemes.

4 Two question correction types that occurred in our data but not in Philp (2003) involved deletion of duplicated forms: (*a*) deletion of a duplicated verb (*Why is he is mad?* → *Why is he mad?*) and (*b*) deletion of a duplicated subject (*Are these people they watching him?* → *Are these people watching him?*).

5 As we will see below, in several cases, only the combined correct and modified recall analysis showed significant differences. But what are the implications of the 'modified' category for the assumptions researchers normally make about acquisition? Our interlanguage analysis assumed that any modification of a learner's trigger utterance is to be considered progress, in terms of acquisition, even when it results in an utterance that is not target-like.

6 At times the researcher had to make a choice about how to formulate the recast based on the context of the participant's utterance. For example, in the case of his use of bare verbs as in (5), the researcher could choose to recast the question either in the present progressive (*Why is he coming...?*) or in the simple past (*Why did he come?*). In such cases, the researcher tried to make reformulations consistent with the time reference frame that had been activated by the speaker in the immediately preceding context.

7 Mackey et al. (2000) found that literate learners also noticed lexical items more readily than morphosyntactic items. We have already noted that semantic language processing seems to be unaffected by literacy; thus, we would expect lexical processing and noticing to be high for both literate and illiterate learners.

8 Earlier versions of parts of Chapter 4 appeared in Bigelow et al. (2006), Tarone and Bigelow (2007), and Tarone, Bigelow, and Hansen (2007). Robert delMas helped considerably with statistical analysis in Bigelow et al. (2006).

5

Working memory and task effects

Working memory[1] is very much a factor in SLA research, but we have not yet said much about what it is or how it functions. Research on working memory has employed tasks like memorization and recall of lists of pseudowords, numbers, and semantically versus phonologically similar words, because the various features of list components are easily controlled. The conditions under which the lists are memorized and recalled can be varied, conditions such as requiring the participant to count backwards during memorization, or to simultaneously perform a manual task during recall. Findings are used to build and then further test models of working memory. These efforts have aided our understanding of how working memory functions, of which aspects of input processing are handled by which parts of the model, and of how input becomes information and then knowledge. Nonetheless, to many of us, these types of tasks may seem artificial and unrelated to the ways we find ourselves using language and memory in the social contexts of everyday life, thus making it hard to see a relationship between working memory research findings and the work we do in SLA research and ESL teaching. In this chapter we will present a brief overview of two major working memory models designed to account for language processing, show how they are related to issues relevant in SLA, and then use these models to discuss the impact of literacy level on the performance of L2 learners on more traditional SLA tasks—first elicited imitation and then recast.

What language processes must memory models account for?

As our brain receives language input, it must temporarily store this input while processing it. During processing, the brain must decode input into meaning (bottom-up processing) and hold it temporarily in working memory while receiving new input (Randall 2007). In addition, in order to interpret the message, our brain must integrate the information with other knowledge (top-down processing) residing in long-term memory. This coordination of bottom-up and top-down processing, resulting in comprehension, is the function of working memory. The best-known model of working memory is Alan Baddeley's (for an entire book devoted to this model, see Baddeley 2007), but numerous other models exist; one of these, the connectionist model, will also be examined here.

Baddeley's working memory model

Alan Baddeley has been researching working memory since the 1960s, and his model has undergone considerable evolution over the years. The basics of Baddeley's current working memory model are that incoming information is stored temporarily in a component that is specialized by modality (visuospatial versus phonological[2]), and that the capacity of these storage components is limited and their contents subject to rapid deterioration (Baddeley 2007). Capacity can be increased by chunking (the bundling of information into units through strong association), and information in the short-term storage component can interact with information stored in long-term memory. Deterioration of information in the temporary store can be slowed by rehearsal. Competition in processing (known in everyday life as 'multitasking') taxes this short-term storage capacity. Allocation of attention between the modality-specific storage components is coordinated by what Baddeley terms the 'central executive'. We can think of Baddeley's model as a specialized multicomponent, capacity-driven, more or less bottom-up processing, trade-off system, where interaction between components is controlled by a central supervisor. This model suggests a serial processing approach, where the order of decoding is sequential—sounds, to words, to sentences (Randall 2007)—and it is also primarily a bottom-up processing model, even as it attempts to account for interaction with long-term memory knowledge. A host of research findings support various aspects of this model. Moreover, it has intuitive appeal: we can all point to problems we have had hanging on to incoming information while multitasking, or to being more oriented to auditory than visual input, or to being able to interpret a received message because of our background knowledge (stored in long-term memory).

Of particular relevance to SLA issues is Baddeley's 'phonological-loop' storage component. The basic function of the phonological loop is to receive auditory input and hold it in storage, through rehearsal, long enough to decode it. Baddeley, Gathercole, and Papagno (1998) propose that the phonological loop is central to language acquisition. While it was clear to them from the beginning that the phonological loop plays a critical role simply in terms of being the locus of incoming phonological information, Baddeley et al. (1998: 170) began to wonder what the impetus for the evolution of such a working memory component in humans would be—certainly not, they said, for 'dealing with phone numbers'. Rather they hypothesized that the primary function of the phonological loop is the 'temporary storage of *unfamiliar phonological forms* [emphasis added] while more permanent memory representations are being built.' As such, the phonological loop had to be a mediator in language learning (Gathercole and Baddeley 1993, as cited in Baddeley et al. 1998: 159). That this component also aids in the short-term memory of familiar verbal material was considered to be 'merely an incidental by-product' (Baddeley et al. 1998: 159). This hypothesized function of the phonological loop could explain the processes and mechanisms involved in childhood language acquisition of sound patterns and, by extension, would have to be critical to learning second languages as well.

Connectionist model

The connectionist models, of which there are several, propose that processing in the brain can occur at several levels simultaneously rather than having to occur in serial order. This processing activity can be visualized as a network of interconnected intersections or nodes where some of the nodes are more important or 'weighted' than others (Randall 2007). During processing, multiple nodes are activated concurrently, based on such factors as the characteristics of the input, the current situation, prior knowledge, and the like. These same factors also affect the level of node activation and node weight. As certain inputs are encountered and processed repeatedly, the weight of specific nodes increases, making them more likely to be accessed during subsequent input processing. Similarly, new nodes may arise, perhaps as chunks constructed from other nodes. Nodes with less or diminishing weight will be activated only when use of more heavily weighted nodes fails to result in a meaningful interpretation of the message. In this way, both processing and learning are distributed across the network, with multiple levels of processing and learning occurring simultaneously. For this reason, the connectionist model is also sometimes referred to as a 'distributed parallel processing' model. While bottom-up processing can certainly be a part of this system, top-down, context- or meaning-based processing is more important. This model also has intuitive appeal. We may recall times when we have processed multiple inputs at multiple levels simultaneously (this may be particularly obvious when listening to a foreign language, when we are more attentive to our processing), or when we knew what someone was going to say well before he said it.

Why do models matter?

Why do these different models of memory and speech processing (and the many others not explored here) matter? If we are interested in the processes of language acquisition, say for diagnostic or pedagogical purposes, then findings from cognitive research may help us do our work. Similarly, if we are researching language acquisition ourselves, we use this model-based cognitive research to help us interpret our results. It is important to understand that there are competing models attempting to explain the same phenomena, that there is overlap in as well as difference between the models, and that the tasks researchers use to test their models have implications for the generalizability of their findings. This last point is particularly relevant for language acquisition research.

Task type considerations

From a language-processing perspective, one of the limitations of the studies described above and earlier in this book is in the task tools they employ: phoneme or syllable segmentation, word and pseudoword repetition. While offering the benefit of experimental control, these tasks are not representative (nor do they claim to be) of the sort of complexity that occurs in everyday language with respect either to utterance construction or to the sociolinguistic environment in which language use occurs. The use of such tasks in SLA research and with low-literacy L2 learners in particular could present problems because of the complex issues involved with storage and access to multiple language systems. But, beyond that, if any of these tasks is to be used for SLA research, then special attention must be paid to the selection of test items to control for L1 versus L2 effects. For example, do the phoneme sequences comprising the test items exist in one, both, or neither language? What is the significance of phoneme features in each of the participant's languages (present, allophonic, or absent)? Are the pseudowords and syllables presented in the study really meaningless in both languages? Certainly, overlap or lack of it between the participant's languages would be another aspect of language experience affecting recall (Coady and Evans 2008). Additionally, sociolinguistic factors, such as discourse constraints inherent in the task, can vary performance from one task type to the next (Tarone 1979, 1985, 2000b; Gass and Selinker 2008). For example, Lantolf and Ahmed (1989) found that the grammatical accuracy of their single participant was higher during an interview task than during a conversation task. Perhaps because of these issues, but more likely because earlier SLA research has been focused on language proficiency and pedagogical issues, language tasks used in SLA research are more contextualized than those that are used in much of memory research. Among these SLA tasks are the recast task with which readers are already familiar (see Chapter 4) and the 'repeat after me' or elicited-imitation task. The characteristics and theoretical implications raised by use of each task type are discussed below.

Elicited-Imitation Task

An elicited-imitation (EI) task is one that requires the participant to repeat verbal stimulus prompts provided by the researcher (Munnich, Flynn, and Martohardjono 1994). The content and structure of the EI prompts can be controlled to highlight what the researcher is examining—for example, grammatical structure, prompt length, and phonemic contrasts. Participant repetitions are transcribed and scored for accuracy. Analysis of EI data may shed light on a range of issues, from child language development and language disorders, to manner of cognitive processing, to working memory capacity, and to L2 proficiency and acquisition.

Most adult SLA research has been directed at gaining insight into the participant's syntactic and lexical L2 development, with occasional attention to working memory considerations. For example, when a meaningful sentence is used as an EI prompt, the nature of the learner's recall accuracy and errors permits inference about the learner's interlanguage rules, his or her comprehension of target language rules, and the relationship between them (Natalicio 1979). An example illustrating this relationship can be drawn from some researcher prompt/participant recall turns in the current study. Here, the prompts are all *do* operator interrogatives:

RESEARCHER	Where do I buy the best donuts?
NAJMA	Where I'm buying best donut?
RESEARCHER	How do you get to the market?
NAJMA	How you get in to market?
RESEARCHER	When does he start work with David?
NAJMA	What time he starting with, with David starting, with the ah work?
RESEARCHER	What do they learn at the movies?
NAJMA	What they lear, learn in the movie?

From the above exchanges, we might infer that the learner comprehends the prompt, based on the lexical and serial order overlap between her repetitions and the target, and that the basic meaning of the prompt is retained in the learner's repetition of it. Note that the participant, Najma, introduces or substitutes morphemes (the contraction of 'am' in 'I'm', the addition of 'ing' to 'buy', the substitution of 'What time he starting' for 'When does he start', for example); these were not presented in the prompts but have syntactic and semantic function, indicating that Najma has comprehended the prompt and is attempting to reproduce it using equivalent forms present in her interlanguage grammar. Notice especially that in every instance, even while the prompt falls within normal short-term memory capacity of 7 ± 2 items before chunking (G. Miller 1956), the learner makes her first error on the second word ('do'), while recalling much of the rest of the prompt. Clearly something more than short-term memory capacity is at work; syntactic processing is also a factor in recall. Because she has consistently omitted the *do*-operator while retaining the *wh* word in each of these recalls, we might infer that, in Najma's interlanguage grammar, *do* support does not exist, and that, in her interlanguage, an initial *wh* word is the sole indication of the question form. An examination of additional interrogative prompt recall data for this participant might support or modify this inference. This is the type of task structuring and analysis of results possible with EI in SLA research.

Still, despite the fact that the above analysis seems logical and is intuitively satisfying, there is disagreement about exactly which skills EI measures and what cognitive processes are responsible for learner imitations. Does EI measure comprehension, productive skills, or simply rote repetition? The gist of the argument for comprehension is that one cannot accurately repeat what one does not understand. Vinther (2002) notes that some researchers argue that EI measures comprehension (Naiman 1974), others that it measures productive capabilities (Eisenstein, Bailey, and Madden 1982), and still others that simple 'parroting' is possible if the string to be repeated is short enough (Lee 1970; Lust, Chien, and Flynn 1987; Munnich et al. 1994). Child language development researcher Ervin-Tripp (1970, as cited in Swain, Dumas, and Naiman 1974) argued that comprehension grammar, as distinguished from production grammar, is a prerequisite for accuracy of recall;[3] she posited a progression from comprehension, to encoding of the input according to the child's own production grammar, to repetition. Naiman (1974), in a study of the SLA of English-speaking children enrolled in a Canadian French immersion program, presented his participants with EI, comprehension, and production tasks. Naiman found that accuracy was best for comprehension (L2 to L1 translation), next best for imitation (EI), and worst for production (L1 to L2 translation). Based on these findings, Naiman concluded that imitation requires both decoding (comprehension) and encoding (production).

Bley-Vroman and Chaudron (1994) discuss EI accuracy not in terms of comprehension and production grammars, but rather in terms of short-term memory capacity and factors that impact it. They propose that the language processor contains multiple discrete levels of representation, such as those in Forster (1987), from least to most complex: visual, letter, syllable, lexical, phrasal, sentence structure, logical form, and interpretative. The language processor automatically attempts to create as complete an input representation across as many levels as possible; the speaker cannot choose which level or levels to use in creation of the representation. They further posit that, while working memory capacity is critical in accurate EI *recall*, it is not a factor in initial creation of the representation for the native speaker (NS), for whom language processing is automatic and self-contained, requiring no short-term memory bandwidth.[4] For the non-native speaker (NNS) still in the process of learning the language, however, they do believe that short-term memory may be used for both L2 processing and storage of the representation, which could potentially impact the quality of both, but that these improve as L2 proficiency grows. Moreover, short-term memory capacity can be extended by chunking, and chunking in turn is facilitated by a grammar-based sentence processor that works on the EI *input*. This would explain why grammatical EI prompts are generally recalled by native speakers more accurately than ungrammatical ones—they are more readily chunked.

In summary, for Bley-Vroman and Chaudron (1994), syntactic processing occurs during the creation of the representation, and it is short-term memory capacity (which capacity is affected by speaker language competence) that affects the accuracy of the recall; it is more of a bottom-up form of processing.

Bley-Vroman and Chaudron (1994) did not examine literacy level as a factor in EI recall accuracy. Indeed, it is interesting to note that, by virtue of its 'letter' level, Forster's levels of representation model (Forster 1987, as cited by Bley-Vroman and Chaudron) explicitly assumes alphabetic literacy. Moreover, the distinction between the letter, syllable, and lexical levels may presume metalinguistic awareness on the part of the learner, an awareness that might not exist with a low literacy level learner. These observations raise questions about how the model could be adapted to account for those who are either illiterate or literate in non-alphabetic orthographies.

Recast Task

The recast task was previously described in detail in Chapter 4 and is recapped here only to facilitate contrast to the EI task discussed above. A recast is corrective feedback consisting of a target-like reformulation by an interlocutor of a non-target-like utterance previously produced by a language learner. For example:

ABUKAR	What did she did? (initial utterance with errors, or 'trigger')
RESEARCHER	What did she do? (recast)
ABUKAR	What did she do? (recall)

As a research tool, a recast task can examine issues similar to those investigated in EI tasks. Unlike the EI task, however, the recast task generally involves an interactive, meaning-focused context. This means that the recasts occur in the context of an activity about something other than just language learning, and that the discussion is collaboratively constructed between the learner and researcher, including not only what is currently being said, but also the cumulative information of the activity, non-verbal cues, and inferences as well (Gumperz 1992). This context is considered important to comprehension and could affect accuracy of recall in general (Jefferies, Lambon Ralph, and Baddeley 2004).

All these threads—short-term memory, and the role of meaning, of output, of task type, and of literacy—come together in interpreting the results of the study described below.

Purpose of the elicited-imitation versus recast study

The goal of this study was to explore the impact of literacy level (the independent variable) on accuracy of interrogative recall across the two task types: EI and recast (the dependent variables). The research questions were:

1 Is literacy level a factor in recall of target sentences in the EI and recast tasks?
  Hypothesis I: The moderately literate group will outperform the less literate group on recall of EI sentences and recast sentences.

2 Is recall of target sentences in EI tasks less accurate than recall of target sentences in the recast tasks?

Hypothesis II: Both literacy groups will perform better on the recast task than on the EI task.

Methodology

Most of the methodology for this study was described in Chapter 3. There are two departures from that methodology in this study, however: the participant pool is slightly different and the method of scoring for accuracy is different. These changes are explained below.

Participants

All but two of the eight participants in the present study are the same as those in the study in Chapter 4. The reason the two sets of participants were not identical is that two of the participants in the study in Chapter 4 were unable to complete the EI task. Two other participants who had completed the task and were matched for mean literacy level to the two they were replacing were substituted. Table 5.1 provides a profile of the EI participants.

Data scoring

Participant recalls for both the recast and EI tasks were assessed for accuracy according to the three-category rubric described below. It is important to note that the rubric used here is different than the one used in Chapter 4. In that study, non-target-like initial participant utterances (triggers) were recast by the researcher, and participant recalls of those recasts were assessed as *correct*, *modified* (part of the target correction is recalled), or *no recall*. That scheme could not be used with the EI recalls in the study reported here, because, with EI, there is no initial non-target-like participant utterance against which a *modified* recall can be judged. Moreover, because this study compared recall accuracy for the two different tasks, the participant's trigger utterance in the recast task cannot figure into accuracy assessment of the recast. Consequently, the accuracy assessment rubric used in this study is not only different from that used in Chapter 4; it also involves a reanalysis of that study's recast data. In other words, the recast accuracy results reported in this EI versus recast study are not the same as those reported in Chapter 4. The current study's rubric, used for both the EI and the recast tasks, has three possible ratings of only the interrogative portion, called here the 'Q-form', of the recall: no recall, grammatical question form, and ungrammatical question form.

No recall means not enough of the target interrogative was recalled for the rater to form an accuracy judgment about it:

RESEARCHER   How do you get to the market?
GHEDI   market

Participant	Age	Gender	Literacy level				Years in USA	Years schooling		Oral proficiency SPEAK rating
			Group	Literacy mean	L1	L2		Pre-USA	USA	
Abukar	15	M	Low	5	4	6	4.5	0	4.5	50
Najma	27	F	Low	5.5	5	6	3	7	1.5	40
Ghedi*	16	M	Low	2.5	0	5	3	0	3	30
Fawzia	20	F	Low	6	6	6	3	0	3	30
Faadumo	18	F	Moderate	9	9	9	3	0	3	40
Moxammed	17	M	Moderate	9	9	9	7	0	7	40
Zeinab*	33	F	Moderate	7.5	8	7	4.5	4	1	30
Sufia	15	F	Moderate	8	9	7	3	0	3	30

* Participants who were not part of the analyses carried out in Chapters 4 and 6.

Table 5.1 Profile of participants in EI task and oral recall analysis

Recalls where the interrogative was grammatical were classified as *grammatical Q-form*:

RESEARCHER   Would you ask if I can attend?
FAADUMO   Will you ask if ah I can /tenay/?

Recalls with ungrammatical interrogative formation were assigned to *ungrammatical Q-form*:

RESEARCHER   Where have the kids been this weekend?
FAADUMO   Where they have the kids been this weekend?

The criteria for assessing the accuracy of the question form focused on whether the recall met a set of syntactic requirements essential to the question form being attempted. This means that a grammatical Q-form recall of the interrogative portion of the target might not match the target exactly, but might still satisfy the syntactic requirements for that type of interrogative. For example, grammatical Q-forms could still have recall errors in elements such as tense, subject–verb agreement, or modal substitution. However, errors in word order, aspect, and some auxiliary usage caused an interrogative to be marked as ungrammatical Q-form. The inter-rater agreement rate for assessing accuracy was 96 percent.

Statistical analysis

As with the recast study described in Chapter 4, exact permutation analysis was used here on both the EI and the recast data. The reader is referred to Chapter 4 and to Hansen (2005) for details. For the current study, recall accuracy was the dependent variable and literacy level the independent variable for both tasks. Because higher literacy level was predicted to produce better recall, one-tailed p-values were reported. To test for significance of difference in performance between the two task types, EI and recasts, a two-tailed paired permutation test was run.

Results

Hypothesis I: The more-literate group will outperform the less-literate group on recall of EI sentences and recast sentences

On the recast task for Hypothesis I, significance was achieved at $p = 0.014$ for the one-tailed test. Literacy level clearly had a positive effect on recall in the recast task. This confirms the findings on recast recall reported in Chapter 4, differences in the recall accuracy rubric and participants for this EI–recast study notwithstanding. The morderately literate group recalled recasts significantly better than the less literate group. As can be seen in Table 5.2, 62 percent of the recast recalls by the low-literacy group were grammatical Q-forms, compared to 77 percent

Participant	Literacy level Group	Literacy mean	Accuracy of Q form EI task No recall %	Raw score	Ungrammatical %	Raw score	Grammatical %	Raw score	Total	Recast task No recall %	Raw score	Ungrammatical %	Raw score	Grammatical %	Raw score	Total	Oral proficiency SPEAK rating
Abukar	Low	5	10	3	45	13	45	13	29	8	3	28	10	64	23	36	50
Najma	Low	5.5	17	5	69	20	14	4	29	11	4	29	10	60	21	35	40
Ghedi	Low	2.5	10	3	45	12	45	13	29	12	4	29	10	59	20	34	30
Fawzia	Low	6	7	2	72	21	21	6	29	3	1	32	12	65	24	37	30
			11	**13**	**58**	**67**	**31**	**36**	**116**	**8**	**12**	**30**	**42**	**62**	**88**	**142**	
Faadumo	Moderate	9	7	2	31	9	62	18	29	4	2	10	5	86	42	49	40
Moxammed	Moderate	9	0	—	24	7	76	22	29	0	—	24	5	76	16	21	40
Zeinab	Moderate	7.5	0	—	45	13	55	16	29	2	1	25	15	73	43	59	30
Sufia	Moderate	8	3	1	62	18	35	10	29	1	1	23	21	76	71	93	30
			2	**3**	**41**	**47**	**57**	**66**	**116**	**2**	**4**	**21**	**46**	**77**	**172**	**222**	
Total by task	**4**	**7**	**16**	**49**	**114**	**44**	**102**	**232**	**4**	**16**	**24**	**88**	**71**	**260**	**364**		

Table 5.2 Accuracy of learner recall of question forms for elicited-imitation and recast tasks

for the moderate-literacy group. Moreover, for every single participant, regardless of the literacy level, the highest percentage of recast recall was in the grammatical Q-form. For the low-literacy group, the spread of grammatical q-form recast scores ranged from 59 to 65 percent; for the moderate-literacy level group, the scores were higher overall, with slightly more spread: 73–86 percent.

An examination of individual participant recast totals reveals that moderate-literacy-group member Sufia appears to be an outlier, in that she had a much higher number overall of recasts (93 compared to 59 for the next closest, Zeinab). Of the four participants in the moderate-literacy group, Sufia had the lowest mean literacy level (8). Both Sufia and Zeinab had the lowest L2 literacy scores (7, see Table 5.1). Both also had received relatively more recasts than the other two moderate-literacy group members, and the lowest SPEAK proficiency ratings (30), so perhaps the number of recasts overall is related to proficiency, although that does not appear to be the case in the low-literacy group, where all participants had a roughly equal number of recasts despite the range in proficiency scores.

On the EI task for Hypothesis I, the one-tailed p-value of 0.057 approached but did not reach significance at $p < 0.05$; the moderately literate group performed better than the less literate group, but not significantly so. Examination of Table 5.2 reveals that, for the low-literacy group, the percentage of grammatical Q-form recalls in the EI task was noticeably lower than the percentage of ungrammatical Q-form recalls: 31 percent grammatical versus 58 percent ungrammatical. The direction of performance was the opposite for the moderate-literacy group with a higher percentage of grammatical recalls (57 percent) compared to ungrammatical (41 percent). Moreover, the percentage of no recalls was much higher for the low-literacy group than for the moderate group (11 percent versus 2 percent). For the low-literacy group, this suggests overall difficulty in recall of the EI prompts, as compared to the moderate-literacy-level group. These findings, coupled with the fact that the exact permutation method has a higher type II (false negative) error rate, bolsters the argument that literacy level may be a factor in group differences.

Individual participant performance on the EI task shows more variation compared to that observed in the recast task. Two low-literacy-level participants (Abukar and Ghedi) have an equal number of grammatical and ungrammatical Q-forms and the other two low-literacy participants have many more ungrammatical than grammatical Q-form recalls. In the moderate-literacy group, every participant except Sufia has more grammatical than ungrammatical EI recalls, with Sufia's data showing not only more ungrammatical recalls, but almost twice as many ungrammatical versus grammatical recalls.

Hypothesis II: Both literacy groups will perform better on the recast task than on the elicited imitation task

Accuracy of recall for recasts was significantly better than accuracy of recall for elicited imitation. The paired permutation test produced a two-tailed

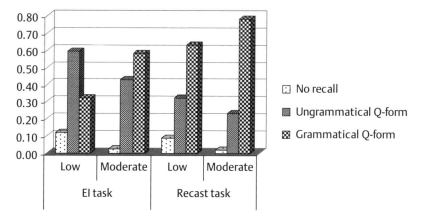

Figure 5.1 Accuracy of recall by literacy level and task type

p-value of *p* = 0.008. A comparison in Table 5.2 of the percentage of grammatical Q-form recalls by task shows that the highest percentages, regardless of literacy level, occurred in the recast task: 62 percent and 77 percent respectively for the low- and moderate-literacy groups. In contrast, grammatical Q-form performance in the EI task was not only lower overall (31 percent for the low-literacy group and 57 percent for the moderate), it was also the reverse direction of that found in the recast task; that is, across literacy groups, there are proportionally more ungrammatical (49 percent) than grammatical (44 percent) Q-form recalls in the EI task than in the recast task (where they are 24 and 71 percent respectively).

Figure 5.1, based on the percentages from Table 5.2, presents a visual summary of results for grammatical versus ungrammatical Q-form versus no recall for both the EI task (on the left) and the recast task (on the right), broken out by literacy level. The *grammatical Q-form* category consists of both perfect recalls and recalls where the syntax of the question form was grammatical but other errors in recall were made. The *ungrammatical Q-form* category consists of recalls where enough of the target was recalled to determine that the interrogative syntax was ungrammatical. The *no recall* category was assigned when not enough of the target was recalled to assess the Q-form. In this figure, the superior performance on the recast task for both literacy level groups is obvious. In fact, accuracy of recall increases stepwise from left to right, starting from lowest (31 percent) for the low-literacy group on the EI task and reaching its peak (77 percent) for the moderate-literacy group on the recast task. And, while the percentages of ungrammatical Q-form recalls are, of course, just the reverse, graphic representation of these results calls attention to how much more difficult both tasks were for the low-literacy group. The fact that the difference between literacy groups on both tasks falls just short of statistical significance, with a one-tailed *p*-value of 0.057, coupled with the risk of Type II error (false rejection of null hypothesis), suggests that even a moderate level of literacy may contribute positively to the ability to recall interrogative syntax in this type of L2 elicited-imitation recall task.

Discussion

There are two primary issues to examine with respect to these results:

1. Why is accurate recall of interrogative forms for both literacy level groups better on the recast tasks than on the EI task?
2. How might literacy level support accuracy of oral recall of the syntactic structure of oral L2 prompts?

The first question will be more easily answered than the second.

The role of context

Why was recall on the recast task so much more accurate than on the EI task? The most obvious possibility is that, because the trigger utterance originated with the learner, comprehension was already accomplished (in contrast to having to decode and comprehend input prior to recall, as in EI). Moreover, the participant had already used his or her production grammar to produce the original utterance. According to Swain's output hypothesis (1995), by virtue of this production, the learner had already formed a syntactic hypothesis. Swain (1995: 126) argues that output facilitates language learner noticing at a conscious level, 'a gap between what they *want* to say and what they *can* say, leading them to recognize what they do not know, or know only partially'), thus causing learners to augment or consolidate existing linguistic knowledge (Swain and Lapkin 1995, as cited in Swain 1995). Taking into further consideration the nature of the recast task, where the object is not just to repeat what is heard, but to correct what one has just said, the participant learner might be cognitively primed to receive corrective feedback and make good use of it.

Another possibility is the presence of context in the recast task. The recast task was contextualized in that the conversation between the learner and interlocutor had a topic focus and visual support in the form of pictures that both parties were viewing. This context meant that there was a core of information that was shared by the learner and the interlocutor. Consequently, things like the identity of referents, location, and event sequence could be assumed rather than explicitly stated between the parties. For example, in the following series of questions from the learner (researcher answers and recasts omitted, learner recalls omitted), the learner was viewing a picture of a man and two women sitting in a row on an airplane.

What he doing, the man sitting in the chair?
What happened there, the woman in the middle sitting?

Why he is looking at her?
What happened there, the girl, she don't know what he looking at?
Where they going?

At first, the learner was fairly specific in his reference to the people in the picture ('the man sitting in the chair', 'the woman in the middle sitting'), but by the third question he had substituted 'he' for 'the man' and 'her' for 'the woman', and by the last question he used 'they' to refer to both of them, and his talk about 'going' was related both to the picture and to events described by the researcher's answers to his questions. This economy of communication might benefit recall in several ways.

Context may promote comprehension. Stories themselves are highly contextualized and recall of even isolated words from stories has been found superior to recall of decontextualized words, a finding attributed to the link between comprehension and long-term memory (Jefferies et al. 2004), or, as observed by Lantolf and Ahmed (1989), what is already 'known' is more readily retrieved. The presence of pictures in the recast task could constitute a form of context and reminder. Tasks involving pictures have been found to improve recall (Dooling and Lachman 1971; Bransford and Johnson 1972; both cited in Jefferies et al. 2004). In the recast task, it could be that the pictures constituted an externalized representation of the comprehended scenario, thus facilitating comprehension of the phonological stream or the focus of attention on non-visually represented aspects of the recast, without loss of the information represented in the picture. In other words, the picture functioned as an anchor, holding the overall context elements while the phonological and syntactic elements in the input received attention.

Doughty (2001) has pointed out that, in order to use the information afforded by the recast, the learner must have sufficient working memory capacity to retain both the target recast utterance and the original interlanguage utterance, or 'trigger'. In terms of memory models, it may be that the presence of shared context reduces the cognitive load the participant has to carry between input of the recast and output of the recall, thus freeing up more processing capacity to attend to noticing the difference between the participant's initial utterance and the recast (something not present in EI). Perhaps also, context promotes chunking. In capacity memory models, chunked data take up less space in working memory and have greater interconnectivity with other knowledge in long-term memory, which in turn leaves more processing capacity available for immediate recall (Baddeley et al. 1998). Similarly, from a connectionist perspective, context might have an effect on the degree of memory activation, and indeed on the level at which information is accessed; that is, top-down processing would be facilitated. As with the capacity models, this would permit more focus on processing less familiar parts of the speech stream and, in the case of the recast task, on finding the differences between the original utterance and the recast and then planning the output.

A final form of context was the utterances of the participants themselves. In the recast tasks the participant had the benefit in most trigger–recast–recall turns of hearing at least some portions of the questions twice or more, which perhaps improved recall by strengthening traces in memory and providing additional opportunities for review and for selective attention, as illustrated below:

SUFIA	Has he answering the phone?
RESEARCHER	Is he going to answer the phone?
SUFIA	Has he is going answering?
RESEARCHER	Is he going to answer the phone?
SUFIA	Is he a going answer to the phone?
RESEARCHER	Is he going to answer the phone?
SUFIA	Is he going answer to the phone?

In this series of trigger–recast–recall turns, Sufia gradually shaped the accuracy of her recall to something closer to the target presented repeatedly by the researcher.

Where the recast tasks provided contextual support and repetition of content, the EI task did not; the participant had no prior idea about the contents of each sentence he or she was asked to repeat and was unlikely to have ever (let alone recently) uttered most of the sentences presented. Moreover, in contrast to the recast situation, each EI sentence to be recalled had no semantic relationship to the previous. These characteristics of the EI task could impair recall by virtue of the absence of exactly those contextual features that facilitated comprehension and recall in the recast task. One might expect that, for non-native speakers of English in particular, L2 recall of decontextualized sentences would be more like recall of pseudowords used in working memory research, in that they have reduced semantic load, thus forcing the learner to rely more on bottom-up phonological processing (Baddeley et al. 1998; Jefferies et al. 2004). This would surely be a disadvantage for less-literate participants, as compared to literate ones, since the literature shows that illiterate participants favor semantic, top-down strategies while literate participants are able to use bottom-up phonological strategies as well. Moreover, even bottom-up strategies in this situation could be compromised because of differences in L1 and L2 phonological systems; the familiar 'context' of one's native phonological structure is absent. And in fact, in the EI task, when these relatively less-literate learners could not recall exactly what was said, their recall attempts were semantically plausible constructions rather than a phonological approximation of the trigger, as can be seen in the following EI responses from different participants:

RESEARCHER	Why does she work late on Sundays?
SUFIA	Why didn't she working last night?
ZEINAB	Why you work later on Sunday?
FAWZIA	Why you /dada/ why you like the Sunday, Sunday?

RESEARCHER	Has he done the driving road test?
SUFIA	Was he driving lesson?
ZEINAB	Has has he /run/ the roads drive license?
RESEARCHER	Have you been to school since Monday?
NAJMA	How how you been since /uh bin/ Monday?
RESEARCHER	Why haven't your friends come to class?
ZEINAB	Why has no friend come to class?
MOXAMMED	Where does your friends come to class?

Note also that, during recall, the meaning of the target may shift. The learners appear to have constructed meaningful sentences around the lexical items they could remember, but, in the process of recall, accuracy in syntactic form and exact meaning were sometimes compromised. In fact, except for the 'no recalls', the recalls were all sentences rather than a jumble of words or word approximations; that is, they exhibited both meaning and syntactic structure, albeit often ill formed.

Context and syntax

While we have already discussed the role of context in supporting recall on the recast tasks, we would now like to consider the cognitive implications in more detail. How might the presence of a context-rich task environment affect recall of syntactic form? Tasks used in working memory studies, as noted in the introductory section of this chapter, compared recall of words and pseudowords, or various permutations of paired associates, such as semantically similar pairs versus semantically dissimilar pairs. These, of course, were disembodied presentations—no context, no syntax. The findings were generally along the lines that word recall was superior to non-word recall, that semantically similar items were more difficult to recall than semantically unrelated pairs; in other words, semantics, or meaningfulness, did affect recall (Baddeley 2007).

What happens to recall when syntax is a factor? Jeffries et al. (2004) cite findings that sentence recall span (capacity) is greater than that of word span, probably because of the involvement of long-term memory (Brener 1940), because the more grammatical and meaningful a sentence the better the recall (Miller and Selfridge 1950), because recall of nonsense syllable sequences bearing grammatical tags was superior to that of untagged sequences (Epstein 1961), and because accuracy of recall for 'anomalous sentences' (grammatically correct but basically meaningless sentences such as 'Noisy flashes emit careful floods') was better than the same sentences presented in random word order (Marks and Miller 1964). In as much as context contributes to meaningfulness, as described earlier, recall of sentences from a higher-context situation should be superior to that from a low-context one, a prediction that is consistent with the current study's findings that recall on the recast task was superior to that of the EI task for both the low- and moderate-literacy-level groups. The question remaining, then, is how does literacy level support recall in general and recall of a syntactic form in particular?

How might literacy support accuracy of recall?

It seems likely, as claimed by Ehri (1993) and Scholes (1998), that the process of acquiring alphabetic literacy in and of itself raises awareness of linguistic forms because these forms are explicitly represented in writing. Therefore, the more literate a person is, the greater the awareness of these linguistic forms and the concomitant strength of that awareness. In the case of accurate recall of the various interrogative forms, perhaps metalinguistically heightened awareness of word boundaries and unstressed words helped the participant decode the input or isolate the change in form required in recall of a recast. Recent brain-scan studies cast an interesting light on possible differences in language processing between illiterate and alphabetically literate persons (Castro-Caldas et al. 1998), and, even more relevant to our concern here, there were differences in the region and level of brain activation depending on whether the person receiving the brain scan was repeating words or pseudowords, and on whether that person was illiterate or literate. Castro-Caldas et al. interpreted these results in terms of literacy-induced differences in cognitive language processing. They explained their finding with reference to a parallel interactive distributed processing (connectionist) model where multiple processing systems are activated concurrently. They postulated that the literate subjects had more processing strategies at their disposal than did the illiterate subjects, and that this level of engagement occurs even when there is no linguistic content, as in pseudoword processing.

In concert with awareness of linguistic form, there might be increased chunking, since the process of representing spoken language in alphabetic script is itself a grouping of sounds into visual representation through graphemes, assembly of graphemes into words, words into phrases, and so on, all reinforced by the availability to the literate learner of dual representation in memory through the visual and auditory modes (Baddeley et al. 1998). This visual tool aids the ability to chunk and could function to increase working memory capacity, prolong rehearsal time, speed up retrieval time, and strengthen connections with long-term knowledge, all of which would result in improved accuracy of recall.

In SLA, literacy may be a particular boon, especially when the learner is confronted with unfamiliar words and sound sequences. It is possible that the moderately literate learner may attempt, consciously or subconsciously, to encode those sound sequences into an alphabetic representation, which, by its very convention, represents a distillation of the speech stream. This representation would serve to aid memory, as described previously, and also to narrow the range of decoding possibilities. In the recast task in particular, the alphabetic representation could function in working memory as an interlanguage token against which subsequent exposure to the same sequence can be compared, in the manner described by Swain (1995). This might be particularly helpful with sublexical morphemes like past-tense markers, as opposed to word-order problems. It may also be in this manner that literacy coordinates with the Baddeley et al. (1998) phonological loop, which they argue is tuned to noticing new, rather than known, sounds, words, and linguistic structures and therefore particularly critical to language acquisition. It could also serve to strengthen particular nodes in the connectionist network, which, as has been discussed earlier, shows more generalized activity in the literate brain.

As pointed out in Swain's output hypothesis, production during the recall process forces the learner to use syntax. Swain argues that output forces 'deeper' and more effortful language processing than does comprehension and has the power to move learners from semantic to syntactic processing (Kowal and Swain 1997; Swain 2000). Metalinguistic reflection can occur when learners directly examine their L2 production, which in turn promotes control and internalization of linguistic knowledge. This, in turn, raises the potential for 'noticing the gap' between what was intended and what actually got said. Inasmuch as alphabetic literacy also raises metalinguistic awareness and possibly clarifies language structure by representing it explicitly, perhaps literacy intensifies the gain or works hand-in-glove with production to maximize noticing and attention to syntactic form. But output may work in yet another way to increase accuracy. The motor theory of speech perception (Liberman, Cooper, Shankweiler, and Studdert-Kennedy 1967; Carroll 1999; both as cited in Randall 2007) hypothesizes that speech perception itself relies on activation of neural processes similar to those involved in speech production. There is support for this from brain imaging, which also shows that speech production areas (central motor area) are activated even when only listening. This implies a connection, perhaps a self-teaching one as hypothesized by the connectionist model, between articulation and perception, and, by extension, to learning an L2. Output then, when coupled with the generalized brain activation found in the literate brain (Castro-Caldas et al. 1998) and the highly contextualized environment of this study's recast task, would work together to promote more accurate recall.

Summary

We began this chapter with an acknowledgement that, while working memory is clearly a factor in language processing, it is sometimes not obvious how working memory research relates to research findings in SLA. This difficulty is due not only to the fact that working memory research is based largely on work with native speakers, but also because the tasks traditionally used seem divorced from 'real' language use in social context and the sorts of tasks used in SLA research. But most importantly, in this chapter we have demonstrated that the type of task employed in research can interact with both a participant's alphabetic literacy level and his or her oral language-processing and production skills. When all this is viewed in concert, we gain a better understanding of the role of literacy and oracy in both SLA and working memory.

Notes

1 While early memory models used the term 'short-term memory', eventually 'working memory' became the preferred term. In this chapter, 'working memory' is used except when citing authors who themselves used the term 'short-term memory', or when the discussion is specifically about a short-term storage component of working memory.

2 Phonological storage is for language-driven input, including both auditory and written input, which is recoded as auditory input. The visuospatial component is associated not with written language, but rather with visual objects and their spatial relationships. In addition, the model contains the episodic component, which blends the visuospatial and phonological inputs (Baddeley 2007).

3 Ervin-Tripp (1970) and Swain et al. (1974) stipulated that the target had to exceed short-term memory capacity (studies of which, at the time, were largely concerned with word and image lists, not syntactically coherent sentences), otherwise rote recall might be possible on grounds of capacity comfort alone. Research since then has laid this issue to rest, and the reasons for doing so are illustrated by the *do* operator examples from study participant Najma presented earlier in this chapter.

4 The language processor may have memory store elsewhere. However, this is beyond the scope of this discussion. What is important according to Bley-Vroman and Chaudron is that, for L1, no short-term memory capacity is posited to be involved in language processing. As they put it, 'the [L1] language processor automatically and obligatorily produces representations of the input and does not itself require the use of short-term memory' (Bley-Vroman and Chaudron 1994: 248).

5 An unpublished earlier version of this chapter appears in Hansen (2005).

6

Literacy level and interlanguage

We have shown in Chapters 4 and 5 that there is a relationship between alphabetic print literacy level and the oral processing of an L2. In the studies reported in those chapters, low-literate L2 learners did not repeat error corrections or perform elicited imitation of L2 questions as accurately as their moderately literate counterparts. These findings suggest that low-literate learners may not notice or process certain aspects of L2 oral input as well as learners with higher literacy skills. These are observations about their oral L2 processing at a single point in time. In this chapter, we ask whether these L2 oral processing differences at a single point in time are paralleled by differences in the L2 grammatical features that the two groups have acquired and use in an oral narrative task. Are the morphosyntactic features of the oral language produced in oral narratives by low-literate and moderately literate L2 learners the same?

To our knowledge, SLA researchers have not studied the relationship between L2 learners' alphabetic print literacy level and the morphosyntactic characteristics of their oral interlanguage. Specifically, there has been no study of the relationship between L2 learners' scores on an empirical alphabetic literacy measure and the specific morphological and grammatical features of their speech.

There are data that may contain clues to the relationship between L2 learners' educational level and their interlanguage (IL) morphosyntax. Both the European Science Foundation (ESF) Project (Perdue 1993) and the ZISA project (Clahsen et al. 1983), in large-scale studies of guest-worker immigrants in Germany, documented their self-reported levels of education in a large-scale study on the grammatical features in their interlanguages. Unfortunately, they did not include a measure of alphabetic literacy level in the battery of tests they asked their L2 learners to perform. Self-reports of years of schooling do not correlate with scores on a good measure of literacy level, but the findings of these studies are interesting, and suggest a possible direction for future SLA research on the interaction between alphabetic literacy level and oral interlanguage.

The ZISA project distinguished two broad types of L2 learners. The interlanguages of the first type of learner contained more 'variational' features of L2, such as semantically redundant grammatical morphemes, while the 'simplifying' interlanguages of the other type of learner lacked these features (Clahsen et al. 1983). Pienemann (2005: 52) reanalyzed these data and classified the ZISA learners into four groups, based on the distribution of fourteen variational features in their interlanguages. These features include such obligatory constituents as subject pronouns, modals, auxiliaries, prepositions, and determiners. (As noted above, many if not all these features are semantically redundant: they are not needed if the speaker is simply trying to be understood.) Pienemann found that these variational features could be distributed among the learner interlanguages implicationally, so that, for example, the learner interlanguage with the 'most highly simplifying feature' also had none of the obligatory constituents listed above.

Processability Theory predicts that these variational features are not affected by processing strategies that are claimed to underlie the universal stages of SLA, stages that cannot be skipped, according to Pienemann's Teachability Hypothesis (Pienemann 2005: 73). Pienemann does not indicate what it is that may have caused the large individual differences in interlanguage construction that were observed in the ZISA study; we do not know why it was that some groups of learners produced interlanguages with so few variational features, while these features were common in the interlanguages of other groups. We do know that different learners in the ZISA group had very different educational levels. It is, therefore, likely that they also varied considerably in the native language literacy levels they had when they entered Germany. Is it possible that their literacy levels were related to different amounts of variational features in their interlanguages? Because the ZISA study did not measure the literacy levels of the learners in their study, and because they did not correlate presence or absence of variational features with self-reported educational level, we do not know.

Do L2 learners with low levels of alphabetic print literacy have fewer variational features in their oral interlanguages? That question is motivated by the following line of reasoning. We saw in Chapter 1 that L2 learners who are not alphabetically literate rely primarily on semantic processing; phonological processing of oral input is more difficult for these learners. Since most of the variational features of interlanguage (Pienemann 2005) are semantically redundant, then they may be less salient, or noticeable, to low alphabetically literate L2 learners who rely only on semantic processing of oral L2. L2 learners who can use alphabetic print literacy to aid them with phonological processing of L2 may be more successful in acquiring these semantically redundant variational features. As a result, the interlanguages of learners with low alphabetic literacy levels may be characterized by fewer variational features than the interlanguages of moderately literate learners. In this chapter, we begin to explore this possibility.

We are also interested in examining the impact of alphabetic literacy level on L2 learners' use of referential expressions such as articles and demonstratives.

Brown, Anderson and Shillcock (1985) have pointed out, based on research, that academically successful and unsuccessful pupils in educational settings handle referential expressions differently. Academically successful students provide more precise reference to entities in narratives, for example, that help listeners keep track of them. We wondered if alphabetic literacy level might be related to this finding. For example, we wondered if lower alphabetically literate learners might omit articles in these narratives even when these might have helped the listener keep track of referents in the stories they told.

Finally, we were interested in finding whether alphabetic literacy level and sentence complexity of interlanguage were related. As mentioned in Chapter 1, Ravid and Tolchinsky (2002) claim that sentence complexity develops with linguistic literacy. In the study reported in this chapter, we wanted to compare the sentence complexity of L2 learners with low and moderate levels of alphabetic literacy, where we operationalized complexity in terms of the use of dependent clauses. However, we also wanted to add a functional component to this comparison, focusing on the learners' use of dependent clauses for a given purpose. The narratives we elicited from our two alphabetic literacy level groups were conducive to the expression of causality in explaining events that occurred in the stories, so we decided to examine whether the learners expressed causality by means of dependent clauses, using subordinating conjunctions like *so* or *because*, as opposed to juxtaposing simple sentences or using some other means that did not require production of complex sentences.

Thus, there were three features of interlanguage that we thought might relate in different ways to the alphabetic literacy levels of these L2 learners: number of variational features in their interlanguages, their use of articles in noun phrases, and their sentence complexity in expressing causality. These are the interlanguage features we focused on:

1 a set of semantically redundant verbal morphemes and plural markers;
2 referential expressions such as articles and demonstratives; and
3 dependent clauses and clauses with *so* that indicate cause and effect.

The relatively small numbers of these features in the story retell database do not permit either definitive conclusions or application of standard statistical measures of significance. Rather, this was an exploratory, qualitative linguistic analysis aiming to identify interlanguage patterns that might be worth studying in more depth in larger-scale future studies.

Research questions

1 Do adults with lower alphabetic print literacy levels supply the same variational interlanguage features in oral narrative tasks as moderately literate learners of a similar background?
2 Is the article use of adults with lower alphabetic print literacy levels in oral narrative tasks different from that of moderately literate L2 learners of a similar background?

3 In expressing causality, do adults with lower alphabetic print literacy levels produce dependent clauses or clauses with *so* as much as moderately literate L2 learners of a similar background?

The narrative data consisted of the story retells elicited via the interactive story-completion task, described in Chapter 3. In this task, after the eight Somali participants had asked the researcher questions about a series of pictures depicting a story, they were shown all the pictures once more and asked to retell the story in their own words. These retells comprise the 'narrative' data that will be analyzed below. Quantitative data will be presented, and illustrative examples will be provided.

Data analysis

Data analysis of the oral narratives that resulted from story retells focused on morphemes used in verb and noun marking, article use in obligatory context, and sentence complexity in expressing causality. The 'variational' semantically redundant grammatical features we examined were the use of bare verbs (that is, verbs with no morphological marking at all) as compared to verbs with morphology, the use of bare nouns (plural nouns without plural morphemes) compared to nouns marked for plural, and the use of articles in obligatory context. To gauge sentence complexity, we compared the two groups with regard to number of relative clauses, noun clauses, and clauses expressing causality.

Results: grammatical forms used in oral narrative

Variational features related to literacy level

Our first research question was: do adult participants with lower alphabetic print literacy levels supply the same variational interlanguage features in oral narrative tasks as moderately literate learners of a similar background? The variational features we investigated were the presence versus absence of verbal morphology (aux *be*, progressive *–ing*, third-person singular present tense *–s*, past tense *–ed*), and presence or absence of plural *–s* on nouns.

Verb marking

The low alphabetic literacy group appeared to produce more bare verbs than the higher literacy group in their oral narratives, though the performance of both groups was variable. Representative examples of third-person singular marking are:

FAADUMO (moderate literacy)   Her mom _says_, 'Come in now, in a car.'
NAJMA (low literacy)   Her mother they _say_, 'We going right now...'

Examples for past tense marking are:

KHALID (moderate literacy)   So, she *called* him.
FAWZIA (low literacy)   Somebody *call* him.

Table 6.1 shows the total number of verbs produced by both groups in their oral narratives, and how many of these were bare verbs—that is, verbs with no verbal morphology. Inspection of Table 6.1 suggests that, while bare verbs were common for both groups, the participants with moderate alphabetic print literacy supplied more verbal morphology on average than the low-literate participants. The low-literate group produced bare verbs 64 percent of the time (205/321), while the moderately literate group used bare verbs somewhat less: 50 percent of the time (230/458). Individuals in the two groups varied in their production of bare verbs. Bare verbs produced by the low-literacy group ranged from 54 percent (50/93) to 77 percent (41/53) and bare verbs produced by the moderate-literacy group ranged from 58 percent (61/106) to 38 percent (45/119). Both groups produced a good number of verbs in their narratives, though the higher alphabetic literacy group produced more: 458 as opposed to the low-literacy group's 321. Given the high variability in the results we found, the relationship between alphabetic print literacy level and use of verbal morphology requires further, more rigorous study.

Noun plural marking

There were fewer obligatory contexts for plural nouns in the story retells than there were for verbs. We wondered whether the low alphabetic literacy group, more than the moderate-literacy group, would use more bare plural nouns,

Participant	Literacy group	Bare verbs in obligatory contexts	Total obligatory contexts	Percentage of bare verbs in obligatory contexts
Abukar	Low	61	95	64
Najma	Low	50	93	54
Ubax	Low	53	80	66
Fawzia	Low	41	53	77
Total		**205**	**321**	**64**
Khalid	Moderate	45	119	38
Faadumo	Moderate	64	115	56
Moxammed	Moderate	60	118	51
Sufia	Moderate	61	106	58
Total		**230**	**458**	**50**

Table 6.1 Bare verbs in obligatory contexts (absence of verb marking)

leaving off the plural –s. There were many bare plural nouns in the data, and the quantitative expression 'a lot of' was used by several participants to mark plural when the plural morpheme was omitted. Representative examples of noun plural marking are:

UBAX (low literacy)   *A lot of monkey_ they take his hat_.*
KHALID (moderate literacy)   *The monkeys took all his hats.*

Table 6.2 shows that the participants with lower alphabetic print literacy levels seemed on average to supply noun plural marking only half the time; 52 percent (36/69) of their plural nouns did not have plural –s. The moderate-literacy group, by comparison, omitted plural –s considerably less on average; only 23 percent (13/57) of their plural nouns lacked plural –s marking. However, individual variation in plural –s marking on nouns was even greater within both groups than was the case with verb marking. The four individuals in the low-literacy group failed to supply plural marking. The range of plural dele-tion was 11 percent (2/18) to 83 percent (19/23). The same range of variation held for the moderate-literacy group, where plural –s deletion ranged from 42 percent (8/19) to 0 percent (0/10). One low-literacy individual did better in marking noun plurals than did three of the moderately literate individuals. Thus, the range of variation overlapped considerably between the two groups, making it highly unlikely that the difference between the mean scores of these groups would be significant, or would allow us to conclude based on these data that noun plural marking is a distinctive feature with regard to alphabetic print literacy. Future studies will need to explore this question further.

Participant	Literacy group	Bare plural nouns in obligatory contexts	Total obligatory contexts	Percentage of bare plural nouns in obligatory contexts
Abukar	Low	2	18	11
Najma	Low	3	12	25
Ubax	Low	19	23	83
Fawzia	Low	12	16	75
Total		**36**	**69**	**52**
Khalid	Moderate	2	16	12
Faadumo	Moderate	0	10	0
Moxammed	Moderate	3	12	25
Sufia	Moderate	8	19	42
Total		**13**	**57**	**23**

Table 6.2 Bare plural nouns (absence of plural marking)

Articles and literacy level

Our second research question was: Do adults with lower alphabetic print literacy levels in oral narrative tasks supply fewer articles in noun phrases than moderately literate L2 learners of a similar background? Here we were examining the use versus non-use of articles in noun phrases mentioning referents in the story retells. The group with moderate levels of alphabetic literacy mentioned marginally more referents (237) than the low-literate group (207).

The target-like use (TLU) of articles in four stories is displayed in Table 6.3. The findings on article suppliance are very mixed. (Following Pica (1983), the formula for TLU is (number correct in obligatory context)/(number of obligatory contexts) + (number of incorrect contexts).) The moderate alphabetic literacy group was more likely than the low-literacy group to use ø article correctly, as indicated by a comparison of TLU (ø). But in the use of the indefinite article, TLU (*a*), the low alphabetic literate group was actually more accurate than the moderately literate group, and use of definite articles was the same by the two groups

Sentence complexity and literacy level

The final research question relates to sentence complexity in expressing causality: Do adults with lower alphabetic print literacy levels produce either dependent clauses or independent clauses with *so* to express causality as much as moderately literate L2 learners of a similar background?

The group with moderate levels of alphabetic literacy seemed to produce more complex sentences in their oral narratives than the group with lower alphabetic literacy. In tabulating the clauses reported in Table 6.4, we did not include those produced in response to a question by the researchers (e.g. 4b below). We counted only those like 4a below, which were attached to another clause uttered by the participant. Similarly, in analyzing independent clauses with *so*, we included those like the first *so* in (*c*) below, where the event reported in the *so*-clause was a logical result of the previous clause. We did not count *so*-clauses that were echoes of the researcher, or that seemed to be used for other meanings (second and third *so* in (*c*) below).

(*a*) ABUKAR (low literacy)	The guy can't talk to her <u>*because*</u> a man between her them them both of them. (A.7–8)	
(*b*) RESEARCHER	How does he know it's not his suitcase?	
NAJMA (low literacy)	<u>*Because*</u> he just said the lady clothes. (A.27)	

Participant	Literacy group	Zero article			Indefinite article			Definite article		
		No. in obligatory context	No. in wrong context	TLU	No. in obligatory context	No. in wrong context	TLU	No. in obligatory context	No. in wrong context	TLU
Abukar	Low	9/10	3	69	7/8	0	88	31/32	1	94
Najma	Low	6/10	12	27	9/12	2	64	35/44	4	73
Ubax	Low	0/0	9	0	11/13	2	73	33/36	1	89
Fawzia	Low	4/5	13	22	1/7	0	14	22/24	4	79
Group Average		**19/25**	**37**	**31**	**24/40**	**4**	**64**	**121/136**	**10**	**83**
Khalid	Moderate	4/4	6	40	5/7	0	71	22/25	0	88
Faadumo	Moderate	4/5	8	31	11/16	9	44	25/37	1	66
Moxammed	Moderate	8/8	4	67	5/7	1	63	56/59	1	93
Sufia	Moderate	6/9	8	35	4/6	3	44	25/31	4	71
Group Average		**22/26**	**26**	**42**	**25/36**	**10**	**54**	**128/152**	**6**	**81**

Notes

[1] For example, Abukar used the zero article correctly 9 out of 10 times in obligatory contexts and used it incorrectly in 3 contexts.

[2] Target-like use (TLU) is number supplied in obligatory contexts divided by number of obligatory contexts plus number supplied in incorrect contexts.

Table 6.3 Target-like use (TLU) of articles (four stories) (*c*) FAADUMO (moderate literacy)   There's a man, he look at his suitcase but it's not his suitcase, but he switch when he <?> right? *So* he is frightened. *So* however he look, *so* someone taking his suitcase. (A.18–23)

Table 6.4 suggests that alphabetic literacy level may have been related to sentence complexity; as a group, the low-literate participants seemed to produce fewer relative clauses, noun clauses, dependent clauses with *when*, and *because*, and independent clauses with *so*, than did the moderately literate participant group. Overall, the moderate alphabetic literacy group used more dependent clauses to express causality than the low-literacy group (131 versus 72). Considering just their use of so-clauses to express causality, we see that the low alphabetic literacy group used fewer (18), while the higher literacy group used more (44). Alphabetic literacy also seemed to be related to use of certain types of clauses more than others. There was a markedly lower use of relative clauses by the low-literacy group (8 as opposed to the higher literacy group's 28 relative clauses).

But these group numbers again obscure considerable individual variation. Within the moderately literate group, three participants produced considerably more dependent clauses overall (34, 33, and 51) than any of the low-literate group; however, the fourth, Sufia, produced fewer dependent clauses (13) than three of the low-literate participants.

Interestingly, individual learners appear to have had definite preferences for certain types of clauses in expressing causality. For example, Table 6.4 shows that, within the moderately literate group, Moxammed preferred relative clauses and 'because' clauses, while Faadumo preferred *so*-clauses.

Participant	Literacy group	Dependent clauses					
		so	*when, because*	Relative	Noun	Other	Total
Abukar	Low	0	14	3	1	2	20
Najma	Low	11	3	2	2	1	19
Ubax	Low	6	10	3	4	0	23
Fawzia	Low	1	8	0	1	0	10
Total		**18**	**35**	**8**	**8**	**3**	**72**
Khalid	Moderate	21	2	5	5	1	34
Faadumo	Moderate	15	9	3	4	2	33
Moxammed	Moderate	8	13	18	6	6	51
Sufia	Moderate	0	6	2	2	3	13
Total		**44**	**30**	**28**	**17**	**12**	**131**

Table 6.4. Dependent clauses used in expressing causality

In spite of this individual variation, however, there appears to be a rather strong pattern in which participants with lower levels of alphabetic literacy produce fewer dependent clauses to express causality. We see this in examining the transcripts in detail. In the example below, both speakers are retelling the same episode in which a man is throwing mangos at some monkeys in order to retrieve the hats they have taken from him. In (*a*), the use of dependent and *so*-clauses allows Khalid, a speaker of moderate literacy, to indicate cause and effect and to do so quite efficiently as compared to Abukar, a speaker of low literacy (*b*), who uses clauses conjoined with *and*. Although both speakers describe the man throwing mangos at the monkeys, only Khalid expresses causality by using *so* to show unambiguously that the man's seeing the monkeys with his hats CAUSED him to throw mangos at them.

(*a*) KHALID (moderate literacy)	He looked up and then he saw *the monkeys wearing them so* he threw a mango *that they threw on a ground that was on it before then* he threw it and they threw a mango at him.
(*b*) ABUKAR (low literacy)	Some monkeys took his hat and try to play with him and now he's right here and try to throw mangos to the monkeys and a monk threw back to um to him um mangos, just laughing.

The pattern seen in the example above may be related to Halliday's distinction (1989) between paratactic structuring common to spoken discourse, and the hypotactic structuring of written discourse. Once again, the individual variation within the small body of data we have prevents us from drawing firm conclusions about the extent to which literacy level relates to the differences we see in (*a*) and (*b*) above. Clearly, this is an area in which we need considerably more research to be done in carefully designed studies, with larger numbers of participants, and reliable measures of both the alphabetic print literacy level of the participants and the syntactic complexity of their oral interlanguages.

Discussion

Alphabetic literacy level had an unclear relationship to the participants' use of variational interlanguage features and articles in their oral narratives. However, there did seem to be a stronger relationship between alphabetic literacy level and sentence complexity in those same narratives. Larger-scale, more in-depth studies must establish whether L2 learners who have low alphabetic literacy achieve oral mastery of variational features and the more complex L2 linguistic forms that are characteristic of written language. There is evidence in L1 acquisition research that children must first be literate before they are able to acquire a set of more complex syntactic structures that characterize written language. Ravid and Tolchinsky (2002) refer to this more complex kind of native language competence as 'linguistic literacy'. According to Ravid and Tolchinsky (2002), linguistic literacy is 'a constituent of language knowledge characterized by the availability of multiple linguistic resources and by the ability to consciously access one's own linguistic knowledge and to view language from various perspectives' (p. 418). Central to this ability is the awareness that 'the kind of language used for writing is essentially different from the one used for speech; and...the perception and growing command of the representational system that is used in the written modality' (p. 418). The sorts of native language syntactic structures acquired with literacy include 'high-register Latinate vocabulary items and connectors, heavy generic noun phrases, passivization for distancing purposes, nonfinite subordination, and complex auxiliary constructions' (p. 429). While simpler syntactic structures are acquired by native-speaking children before they become literate, the authors argue that there is a set of more complex syntactic structures (such as those identified by Biber (1988) and Biber et al. (2002) as characterizing the use of language for literacy) that may not be acquired in one's *native* language until after several years of literate experience. With native language acquisition, of course, it is unclear whether this late acquisition of more complex syntax results from simple maturation, or is somehow related to the addition of literacy. Ravid and Tolchinsky make the strong case that it is a result of literacy. And the results of research on older children and teenagers suggest that 'simple maturation' alone does not always result in more complex syntax; see Yule (1997), as well as Romaine (1984) and Karmiloff-Smith (1986).

　The claim that acquisition of certain more complex syntactic structures of the native language depends on literate experience raises a similar possibility, for SLA. While some L2 forms may be accessible to adult learners with minimal alphabetic literacy, just as similar L1 forms are to child learners who are not alphabetically literate, some more complex syntactic structures (those acquired with 'linguistic literacy') may benefit from, or even require, a base level of alphabetic print literacy. This possibility suggests that we may find that adult L2 learners whose alphabetic literacy levels are minimal or low still become quite fluent using relatively simple syntactic structures. They may learn to use semantic and lexical strategies in a sophisticated way to use those simple syntactic structures to achieve higher-level pragmatic and sociolinguistic goals. Many of the participants in our study seem to fit this exact profile: they are fluent in their L2, they use it in pragmatically adept ways, they are strategically skilled. And yet those with lower alphabetic print literacy skills appear to be less adept at noticing oral corrective feedback on certain language forms, and appear to use less-complex L2 syntax and fewer variational features. They may require higher levels of alphabetic literacy to learn to use these linguistic features of English, their L2.

Summary

Chapter 6 has presented preliminary data on the relationship between alphabetic literacy level and the interlanguage forms produced in oral narratives by low-literate adult learners of English L2. Our preliminary findings suggest that the learners with lower levels of alphabetic literacy produced more bare verbs and unmarked nouns, and fewer dependent clauses than the moderately literate learners. A question our research raises for the SLA field is whether alphabetic literacy level is related to learners' pursuit of a 'simplifying' path of SLA (omitting variational features of the target language) versus an 'elaborating' path (supplying those features). It also raises the question whether full mastery of the syntactic structures in English L2 requires some minimal level of alphabetic print literacy.[1]

Note

1 The analysis reported in Chapter 6 was first carried out with Bonnie Swierzbin, and an earlier version of the results was published in Tarone, Swierzbin, and Bigelow (2006).

7

Implications for research and pedagogy

The research presented in this book has a number of important implications, both for SLA research and theory, and for educators of adolescent or adult students with little alphabetic print literacy who are learning a new language.

Implications for existing SLA research agendas

The first and most important implication for the existing SLA research agenda is that we need more research on the ways in which alphabetic literacy level affects oral SLA, because this work is far from complete. As a field we need better, more thorough measurements of alphabetic literacy for L2 learners, especially at the very beginning levels, so that we can better identify L1 and L2 skills and find relationships to oral language use across a continuum. The Native Language Literacy Screening Device, used with the rubric in Appendix A, worked reasonably well for us, but we are sure better measurements can be developed. We ask readers to draw on their own expertise both to envision how to extend the literature we have reviewed to the field of SLA as well as imagine what our findings mean in the language-learning contexts they know best.

The research we have synthesized in Chapter 1 shows that adults who have not mastered an alphabetic script have both strengths and weaknesses in language use. They have specific strengths in their oral language processing: the ability to rhyme and perform phonemic discrimination tasks, and the ability to acquire new lexical items efficiently. The Somali participants in our studies come from a culture that draws on ancient oral traditions of reciting and improvising poetry, telling stories, and memorizing long passages from the Quran. These powerful traditional oral language uses continue in communities within the Diaspora and have naturally expanded to include topics of today as well as new genres such as hip-hop poetry. Our personal experiences mirror those of so many educators we know who remark about how quickly Somali young people learn to speak English and how skilled they often seem in their interpersonal and pragmatics skills. Some of these strengths may be grounded in Somali culture, and some may be attributed to the strategies a low-literate individual develops to navigate in a highly literate society, such as developing strategies to memorize a lot of information purely through the oral modes.

The research presented in Chapter 1 identifies oral language tasks where adults with no alphabetic literacy do as well as adults who are alphabetically literate: semantic fluency tasks, where they list words drawn from a semantic class, repetition of meaningful words, and rhyming tasks. But this research also suggests that adults who are not alphabetically literate have particular weaknesses in processing language orally; they rely on semantic processing almost exclusively, without the aid of the phonological segmentation skills deriving from alphabetic literacy. For example, in comparison to alphabetically literate adults, they have more trouble repeating pseudowords (words with phonological form but no meaning) and listing words that begin with the same phoneme, manipulating phonemes by adding or deleting them, or reversing phonemic order. They have similar difficulty manipulating syllables: deleting them, or reversing their order. The researchers reviewed in Chapter 1 conclude that alphabetic literacy provides adults with additional cognitive tools to draw upon when they are required to process their native-language oral input in terms of its linguistic form.

Our findings show the relevance of this research for SLA. In this book, we show that alphabetic literacy level is significantly related in similar ways to difficulties adolescents and adults have in processing oral L2. For example, when the L2 learning participants in our study received corrective feedback that involved reversing word order, their alphabetic literacy level was significantly related to their uptake. Indeed, what the less literate participants noticed in the SL input, which included interaction and explicit/implicit feedback, appeared to differ from what the moderately literate learners noticed. Just as in the studies reviewed in Chapter 1, the lower their alphabetic literacy level, the more they appeared to focus on the semantic elements of the communication, rather than the morphosyntax of the language; they also seemed to notice changes in stress pattern before noticing changes in word order.

These preliminary findings suggest that both the strengths and the weaknesses of adolescents and adults who are not alphabetically literate need to be explored at much greater length. Simply put, we need to know more about how they process an oral L2 to gain a fuller picture of the role of alphabetic literacy in oral SLA, and hence of the human capacity for language processing and acquisition. Our findings thus far suggest that alphabetic literacy may be a very important variable in the acquisition of oral L2 skills, but this variable has not yet been adequately explored in SLA research.

The theoretical implications of the claim that alphabetic print literacy affects adults' processing of oral L2 cannot be ignored; research is needed to probe the scope and validity of several core constructs in SLA. Below we list some of the research questions that have occurred to us; we are sure our readers will think of others.

Does the noticing hypothesis apply to adolescent or adult learners who are not alphabetically literate?

1 Do learners who are not alphabetically print literate have to notice L2 forms in order to acquire them?
2 If so, what does it take to get a learner who is not alphabetically literate to notice L2 forms that must be noticed in order to be acquired?
3 Do all L2 forms have to be noticed by learners who lack alphabetic literacy before they acquire them, or just some? Which ones?
4 Does corrective feedback have to be provided to learners who are not alphabetically literate in different ways in order to affect acquisition?
5 Does a learner's relative level of alphabetic print literacy have a differential effect upon the answers to questions 1–4 above?

Does alphabetic literacy level affect working memory for L2?

1 Do L2 learners who are not alphabetically literate organize working memory in terms of stress, rhythm, and rhyme instead of linguistic units?
2 Do L2 learners who are not alphabetically literate organize working memory in terms of vocabulary and semantic classes instead of linguistic units?
3 Does the system of organization of working memory of L2 learners who are not alphabetically literate permit them to acquire the more complex syntactic patterns that normally are learned through reading?

How does alphabetic literacy level affect implicit and explicit L2 processing and learning?

1 Do L2 learners who are not alphabetically literate rely on implicit cognitive systems in learning L2?
2 If so, are they more successful in acquiring some aspects of L2 than literate learners who must convert explicitly processed input into implicit knowledge?
3 If not, is there any difference between L2 learners who are and are not alphabetically literate in their use of explicit cognitive systems in SLA?

Does alphabetic print literacy level affect the L2 forms that are acquired over time?

1 Does the Multidimensional Model/Processability Theory apply to adult L2 learners who are not alphabetically literate? Do illiterate and literate learners follow the same developmental stages of SLA?

2 Does alphabetic literacy level affect an L2 learner's tendency to omit variational features (follow a simplifying path) rather than supply them (follow an elaborating path)?

3 How long does it take an adolescent or adult who has low alphabetic literacy to reach a threshold of phonemic awareness that supports the ability to notice corrective feedback?

4 Does alphabetic literacy level affect an L2 learner's ability to acquire complex syntax, or 'linguistic literacy', particularly the kinds of syntactic patterns commonly found in academic genres, such as relative clauses, passives, and complex NP and VPs?

In pursuit of answers to questions such as these, we hope more SLA researchers will embrace the benefits of doing research with understudied populations in community as well as classroom settings. Broadening the scope of *who* we study will add new knowledge to our field. If alphabetic print literacy level or the amount of formal schooling is to be a key distinguishing characteristic of the individuals studied, there must be instrumentation that clearly delineates and defines such characteristics. We need to be able to operationally identify the alphabetic print literacy levels of our participants, both in L1 and L2. If multilingualism, bidialectalism, oral language strengths, or language/learning disabilities are new focuses of research into understudied populations, all these characteristics must be fully problematized, operationalized, and described via carefully thought-out research designs.

A new SLA research agenda: Studying SLA and L2 use in social context

Although the research questions we outline above are important extensions of the *existing* SLA research agenda, we return now to our position, stated at the beginning of this book, that the existing research agenda is seriously limited in that it constructs SLA as an abstract cognitive process that is unaffected by social context. The studies reported in this book are replications of this same type of study: though we carried out those studies in a non-traditional population, and, we hope we did so in a culturally sensitive way, our replications still made essentially the same assumptions as the original studies.

What we did not do in those studies was to examine the way these learners engaged in SLA in their own worlds, in their own social contexts. If we are to study the process of SLA engaged in by all kinds of L2 learners in a range of social contexts outside schools and academia, then we will need to reconceptualize the research enterprise. We need to study SLA as L2 use and development in real social contexts, and not just treat IL as an abstract system.

We must continue to expand our research horizons if we are truly to understand the L2 learning processes of Somali refugee communities and others like them. Our experience in Somali communities in Minnesota has led us to see that learning about their communities and cultures leads to even more questions that are probably relevant to many other immigrant or refugee groups from societies different from our own or those we know. Knowing more about them, and their language learning in and out of classroom settings, can only help to make their educational experiences better—both socially and academically. Future research in this community that constructs SLA as L2 use in real social contexts, not as an abstract system, should consider the impact of the following factors, and address the following research questions. Addressing these questions will require an expansion of the existing SLA research enterprise.

Out of school literacies

Adolescents and adults use language and literacy (including digital literacies) in many ways outside the classroom, For example, in many Somali families, children study the Quran with a *duksi* or tutor and develop literacies related to these experiences, albeit not typically valued at school. Children learn to recite from the Quran,[1] and many Somali youth with very low Somali and English print literacy are able to match sounds to Arabic letters and pronounce long passages of the Quran (but not read for comprehension). How do these skills bridge to English literacy learning in formal classroom settings? How do youth use their developing English language and literacy skills for religious purposes outside school?

Somali communities and the Diaspora

Somalis may be unique among immigrant groups in that they have a strong clan and kinship system that continues to be important both in Somalia and among some communities in the Diaspora. The clan system is a reliable form of socio-economic security and is still intact, in part because of the absence of reliable state institutions. It has traveled with Somalis into Diaspora societies, including the one in Minnesota, undoubtedly to solve different problems and meet different needs. 'Somalis will continue to cling to the only system that has worked for them since time immemorial' (Abukar Ali, May 25, 2008, personal communication). Regardless of clan ties, Somali communities in Minnesota seem very well connected through traditional means (word of mouth) as well through radio and television programs. If we assume this is true, how does this important source of social capital influence the need for maintaining strong Somali language skills, or developing strong English language skills? How is language used among Somalis who live in countries around the world? Does local and global networking depend on digital literacies, and if so, how does it function?

Interrupted formal schooling

Many, many Somalis living outside Somalia have had the harrowing experience of fleeing Somalia and have then lived in refugee camps for long periods of time.[2] These camps were and continue to be places of scarcity, disease, and violence. The experience of being a refugee has caused many Somali newcomers to experience interrupted schooling. While there had been few Somalis in school before 1990, after 1990 there were even fewer. Given these facts, we expected in 2004–5, when we collected the data for these studies, that most of the adolescents and young adults we would meet would probably never have attended school. This expectation was upheld by our participants and confirmed through personal accounts from teachers. Many questions arise with respect to interrupted formal schooling. What exactly were the educational opportunities in the refugee camps? What experience did refugees have of learning languages from other refugees (for example, Arabic, Nubian) or from individuals from the host country (for example, Amharic, Swahili)? If they acquired print literacy from elders in the camps, how were they taught? What texts did they read or write? Which oral or written texts were valued and protected during displacement?

Oral traditions

Somalia has rich oral traditions that are centuries old. Somali stories, dramas, jokes, proverbs, and poems are an important part of the culture, traditional and contemporary. Poets in particular enjoy immense prestige in Somali society, a fact that has surprised outsiders from the nineteenth century to the present. Poets are usually deeply involved in current public affairs, even attempting to influence their course (Andrzejewski 1988). An appreciation for modern-day poets is alive and well in the Somali community in Minnesota. There is poetry that is recited by men (*gabayga ragga*), and poetry that is recited by women (*buraanburka dumarka*). There are poetry contests (*gabay-ku-dood*) and poetry chosen for special occasions. Poetry is still improvised for Somali weddings in Minnesota (Abukar Ali, personal communication, April 7, 2008).

The oral genres that pervade Somali society are a valued type of literacy. Their rhetorical structures include plays on words, rhymes, and rhythms. Some oral texts are memorized through the use of mnenomic devices such as alliterative verse that follows complicated traditional patterns.[3]

Oral traditions continue to be important in the Diaspora. K'Naan, a Somali rapper from Toronto, is an excellent example of a contemporary Somali poet. The language used is English, and the messages are about current problems of racism and injustice, but his role and his craft seem timeless and fitting of Somali oral traditions in that he uses language to mobilize public opinion as well as to agitate for different causes. Following in the footsteps of the Somali poets before him, he comments on public affairs, including issues such as the United Nations' failed relief effort in Somalia. In an interview (Dickie 2005), he was quoted as saying:

> The focus has always been the message, the words, what you've got to
> say....In Somalia you don't necessarily have to be a good singer or have a

good sound, but you have to have something moving to say. That's what a successful musician is in Somalia. And there have been times when words have literally caused the condition of the whole country to shift. When colonialism was ousted from my country, that revolution was not led by a militant guy but by a poet...and in the '40s my grandfather was credited with stopping a war between two clans with one single poem. That's the way it is there.

Relevant SLA research questions to be explored here include, but are certainly not limited to, the following:

1 What are the oral genres used by Somalis with limited print literacy?
2 How are these genres used outside Somalia and how are they influenced by increasingly multilingual and multiliterate communities of speakers?
3 Are the skills developed in using these traditional Somali oral genres used by Somalis in acquiring English?

Language and identity

Language learners have great agency in their use of the English L2 (Ibrahim 1999; Bashir-Ali 2006). We would expect language use to reflect the social context in terms of what language variety has prestige or power. How does this shift over time among the immigrant community and across generations? It should also be expected that immigrants and refugees are using language in new ways that mirror their hybridized lives and changing identities. How does a range of inter- and intra-ethnic interaction influence language choice and use? Do these uses of language involve code-switching? How do digital literacies such as text messaging or blogging provide multilingual spaces for newly literate adolescents and adults? Who do newly literate adolescents or adults speak or write to, and in what language(s), and how do they show audience awareness? How do language learners use language to assert a chosen identity in a society that lumps them together with other phenotypically 'black' people? How does a gendered or religious identity matter in terms of valued literacies? Issues such as national, racial, ethnic, gender, and religious identity must be explored in the light of language use and acquisition.

Negotiating communication in classroom settings

The research we read, as well as the research we carried out ourselves, was not conducted in classroom settings. The implications of this are many. For instance, we do not know what lack of alphabetic literacy means for instructed SLA in heterogeneous high-school or adult basic education classes. How do immigrant and refugee adolescents and adults who are not alphabetically literate experience content learning in classes only partially designed to meet their needs? What can and do they learn through the oral modes about academic content as well as about language in such settings? Many, many questions remain about how refugees and immigrant students without alphabetic literacy are welcomed or not welcomed into the social fabric of schools, which frames their contexts of language use, and their ability to imagine taking on a new identity as a literate, schooled individual in a society where this has much practical and symbolic value.

Including minority researchers

We hope that researchers will act responsibly as they move into this unknown territory. It would be beneficial for the field if there were more scholars from minority communities who could move within and between communities with greater sensitivity. For outsiders, like us, it was important to take the time to learn about the Somali communities of our area and to participate in activities that brought us into meaningful contact with youth, community leaders, and parents, some highly educated and others not at all. We learned how invaluable community partners can be for facilitating access and advising on many phases of a research project.

Implications for pedagogy

In terms of what the research presented in this book means for educators, we wish to be cautious. The most conclusive observation we can offer educators is that we are certain that older language learners who lack alphabetic print literacy are using the linguistic input they receive orally in different ways from those who are alphabetically literate. Given what our Somali participants can do in their L2, perhaps less time needs to be spent on developing-fluency activities compared to accuracy activities. On the other hand, it is useful to know that learners with very low alphabetic literacy may have difficulty perceiving oral corrective feedback that requires a particular focus on or manipulation of word order. We do not know how they perceive corrective feedback targeting morphemes or phonemes. But, as alphabetic literacy develops, it is presumed that these skills would develop and therefore become a useful processing tool.

The implications of this work for how to teach reading of an alphabetic script are unclear at this time, so we will make only some global comments here. We believe, as we always have, that a balanced literacy approach is appropriate. Like all beginning readers, adolescent and adult English-language learners must be taught both how to decode and encode an alphabetic script, and how to engage in intensely meaningful and age-appropriate literacy activities that have purpose. Our study showed that our participants who had low alphabetic literacy did better on oral tasks that were contextualized, like the recast tasks, than on oral tasks that were not, like the elicited imitation tasks. This suggests to us that alphabetic literacy activities will be more successful if they too are contextualized. In addition to understanding and learning the phonological significance of letters in an alphabetic script, we believe, like Adams and Bruck (1994: 105) that

> it is vital that literacy development involve reading, and writing, and spelling, and language play, and conceptual exploration, and all manner of engagement with text, in relentlessly enlightened balance.

There is an advantage in teaching students who have a great deal of oral language fluency in the L2 how to read that language: as they learn to decode, they can more easily make meaning of the text. This type of learner stands in stark contrast to so many who know how to make sound–symbol correspondences, but, upon 'decoding', do not arrive at words or sentences that they can comprehend.

Given our participants' relative oral language strengths and weak alphabetic literacy skills, it is likely that any pedagogical tools that build connections between oral and written modalities and media would be fruitful. We have seen teachers build such connections by encouraging students to engage their rhetorical knowledge of oral language genres such as poetry and folktales from their native language to encode similar texts in English. Bridges into academic texts could be made through lessons that include the teacher or peers reading aloud, thinking aloud, discussing, and gradually helping students to their own oral and written representations of academic concepts. These meaningful, purposeful top-down approaches to literacy involving multiple genres will be effective in building background knowledge and making literacy instruction enjoyable to adolescent or adult learners. However, it is essential to offer learners who are not literate in an alphabetic script systematic instruction in connecting sounds with letters and groups of letters, blending sounds together, and learning to recognize patterns in words. We believe that it is appropriate to ask adolescents and adults to memorize high-frequency words and words that do not follow typical patterns (that is, sight words). Developing the skills to make grapheme–phoneme correspondences and to identify word boundaries usually requires explicit instruction, but these skills can be taught in meaningful contexts and within a curriculum that also builds literacy through top-down practices that connect oral language strengths to the written word.

Call for research

It is extremely important for SLA researchers to carry out future large-scale or in-depth studies to identify both the syntactic structures and the pragmatic strategies that are used orally by adolescent and adult L2 learners who have minimal or no alphabetic print literacy. We need to know whether and how the language and alphabetic literacy processing skills they have enable or impede them as they seek to attain their own vocational and academic goals. It is imperative that SLA researchers explicitly include as a focus of study L2 learners whose alphabetic print literacy skills are absent or low, that they consider those skills central to research design in future SLA research studies, and that they design these studies so as to explore the language use and SLA processes of these learners in a range of social contexts.

Notes

1 For example, in 2005, a 12-year-old Somali girl won a competition in Mogadishu for memorizing the entire Quran (Cassanelli and Abdikadir 2007).

2 According to United Nations High Commission on Refugees (UNHCR), as we write in 2008, there are 50,000 Somali refugees in Mombasa, Kenya, 150,000 in the North Eastern Province of Kenya, and 400,000 Somali refugees in eastern Ethiopia. There are approximately 100,000 refugees and asylum-seekers who have fled violence and persecution at home and live in or around Nairobi. There are at least 270,000 additional refugees who live in Kenya's two refugee camps, Dadaab, near the Somali border, and Kakuma camp, near Sudan's border (Chanoff 2008).

3 For example, 'a gabay poem has long lines of 20 morae each, of which 12 occur in the first hemistich and 8 in the second, with a caesura which has to coincide with a word boundary' (Andrzejewski 1988: 8). Every line must contain at least one alliterative word and the same alliteration has to be maintained throughout the poem. This requirement places huge demands on the lexical resources and inventiveness of the poet, who may need to find 400 words beginning with the same alliterative sound for a poem of 200 lines (Andrzejewski 1988).

Appendix A. Literacy rating scale

Rating	Native Language
	Reading fluency
1	Follows with pen; much sub-vocalization; slow speed; retraces/backtracks; much comprehension difficulty;* asks researcher for help.
2	Starts out slowly and then speeds up, still showing some difficulty in decoding; may follow with pen or finder and/or sub-vocalize; often reads twice, much faster the second time.
3	Very comfortable; little sub-vocalization; speed relatively quick; little comprehension difficulty;* may comment on perceived orthographic errors in the Somali text.

	Writing
1	Writes in another language, can/will not write in native language.
2	Writes laboriously in native language; may complain about not knowing how to spell; sub-vocalizes; may ask for help.
3	Writes in native language without any hesitation.

	Confidence
1	Expresses reluctance to read or write in native language; may say cannot do it.
2	Will try, but not very sure of skills; asks questions along the way.
3	Approaches task without hesitation.

Rating	Second language
	Reading fluency
1	Follows with pen; much sub-vocalization; slow speed; much comprehension difficulty.*
2	Starts out slowly and then speeds up, still showing some difficulty in decoding; may follow with pen or finder and/or sub-vocalize.
3	Very comfortable; little sub-vocalization; speed relatively quick; little comprehension difficulty.

	Writing
1	Writes in native language and cannot/will not write in second language.
2	Writes laboriously in second language.
3	Writes in second language without any hesitation and few orthographic errors.

	Confidence
1	Cannot tackle a single word.
2	Will try but not very sure of skills; asks questions along the way.
3	Approaches task without hesitation.

* Evidenced by responses to researcher questions.

Appendix B. Elicited-imitation sentences

Stage*	Short interrogative sentences
5	Where do I buy the best donuts?
6	Why hasn't your friend come to class?
4	What is the name of the teacher?
5	What is the new drug store selling?
4	Is she nice to the young children?
6	Would you ask if I can attend?
5	How do you get to the market?
6	It is a new car, isn't it?
5	When are they coming to St Paul?
4	Are the green apples a good price?
6	She went to the nurse, didn't she?
6	Who didn't they ask to the game?
4	How are Tom's new friends from Hopkins?
5	When does he start work with David?
4	Have you been to school since Monday?
6	Can you explain who that man is?
5	Who will he live with in Roseville?
5	What do they learn at the movies?
4	Why were the kids sad on Friday?
5	Why has she gone to complain there?
6	Why didn't she drink the sweet tea?
4	When is the next big soccer game?
6	Can you explain where the bank is?
4	Are you starting a new job search?
5	Why does she work late on Sundays?
4	Has he done the driving road test?
5	Where have the kids been this weekend?
6	You like the apple cake, don't you?

* Stage of acquisition as developed by Pienemann and Johnston (1987) and Pienemann et al. (1988).

References

Adams, M. J., and M. Bruck. 1994. 'Word recognition: The interface of educational policies and scientific research'. *Reading and Writing: An Interdisciplinary Journal*, 5: 113–39.

Adrian, J. A., J. Alegría, and J. Morais. 1995. 'Metaphonological abilities of Spanish illiterate adults'. *International Journal of Psychology*, 30: 329–53.

Afrah, M. M. 2004. 'Somalis in America, two thumbs up'. August 12. Retrieved on March 20, 2008, from http://www.banadir.com/somalis_in_america.shtml.

Ammar, A., and N. Spada. 2006. 'One size fits all? Recasts, prompts and L2 learning'. *Studies in Second Language Acquisition*, 28: 543–74.

Anderson, J. R. 1982. 'Acquisition of cognitive skill'. *Psychological Review*, 89: 369–406.

Andrzejewski, B. W. 1988. 'Infills: Nouns and verbs without lexical meanings in Somali oral poetry'. *African Languages and Cultures*, 1/1: 1–14.

Baddeley, A. 1986. *Working Memory*. Oxford: Oxford University Press.

Baddeley, A. 1990. *Human Memory: Theory and Practice*. Mahwah, NJ: Lawrence Erlbaum Associates.

Baddeley, A. 1995. 'Working memory', in M. S. Gazzaniga (ed.), *The Cognitive Neurosciences*. Cambridge, MA: MIT Press.

Baddeley, A. 2003. 'Working memory and language: An overview'. *Journal of Communication Disorders*, 36: 189–208.

Baddeley, A. 2007. *Working Memory, Thought, and Action*. Oxford: Oxford University Press.

Baddeley, A., S. E Gathercole, and C. Papagno. 1998. 'The phonological loop as a language learning device'. *Psychological Review*, 105: 158–273.

Bashir-Ali, K. 2006. 'Language learning and the definition of one's social, cultural, and racial identity'. *TESOL Quarterly*, 40: 628–39.

Ben-Dror, I., R. Frost, and S. Bentin. 1995. 'Orthographic representation and phonemic segmentation in skilled readers'. *Psychological Science*, 6: 176–81.

Berman, R. 2002. 'Peer commentary on "Developing linguistic literacy: A comprehensive model" by Dorit Ravid and Liliana Tolchinsky'. *Journal of Child Language*, 29: 453–7.

Berthoud-Papandropoulou, I. 1978. 'An experimental study of children's ideas about language', in W. J. M. Levelt, A. Sinclair, and R. J. Jarvella (eds.), *The Child's Conception of Language*. Berlin: Springer-Verlag.

Bialystok, E. 1981. 'Some evidence for the integrity and interaction of two knowledge sources', in R. Anderson (ed.), *New Dimensions in Second Language Acquisition Research*. Rowley, MA: Newbury House.

Biber, D. 1988. *Variation across Spoken and Written English*. Cambridge: Cambridge University Press.

Biber, D., and M. Hared. 1991. 'Literacy in Somali: Linguistic consequences'. *Annual Review of Applied Linguistics*, 12: 260–82.

Biber, D., R. Reppen, and S. Conrad. 2002. 'Developing linguistic literacy: Perspectives from corpus linguistics and multi-dimensional analysis'. *Journal of Child Language*, 29: 458–62.

Bigelow, M. 2007. 'The social and cultural capital a Somali teen brings to school', in N. Faux (ed.), *Low-Educated Second Language and Literacy Acquisition: Research, Policy and Practice. Proceedings of the Second Annual Forum*. Richmond, VA: Literacy Institute at Virginia Commonwealth University.

Bigelow, M. 2008. 'Somali adolescents' negotiation of religious and racial bias in and out of school'. *Theory into Practice*, 47: 27–34.

Bigelow, M., R. delMas, K. Hansen, and E. Tarone. 2006. 'Literacy and the processing of oral recasts in SLA'. *TESOL Quarterly*, 40: 1–25.

Blanco-Iglesias, S., and M. Broner. 1997. *Methodological and Ethical Issues in Classroom-Based Research*. CARLA Working Paper #6. Minneapolis: Center for Advanced Research on Language Acquisition, University of Minnesota.

Bley-Vroman, R., and C. Chaudron. 1994. 'Elicited imitation as a measure of second-language competence', in E. Tarone, S. M. Gass, and A. D. Cohen (eds.), *Research Methodology in Second-Language Acquisition*. Hillsdale, NJ: Lawrence Erlbaum Associates.

Bondevik, S. 1996. 'Foreigner talk: When does it occur and why?' Paper presented at the Eleventh World Congress, International Association of Applied Linguistics (AILA), Jyväskylä, Finland.

Bransford, J., and M. Johnson. 1972. 'Contextual prerequisites for understanding: Some investigations of comprehension and recall'. *Journal of Verbal Learning and Verbal Behavior*, 11: 717–26.

Brener, R. (1940). 'An experimental investigation of memory span'. *Journal of Experimental Psychology*, 26: 467–82.

Brown, G., A. Anderson, and R. Shillcock. 1985. *Teaching Talk: Strategies for Production and Assessment*. Cambridge: Cambridge University Press.

Carpenter, H., K. S. Jeon, D. MacGregor, and A. Mackey. 2006. 'Learners' interpretations of recasts'. *Studies in Second Language Acquisition*, 28: 209–36.

Carr, T. H., and T. Curran. 1994. 'Cognitive factors in learning about structured sequences: Applications to syntax'. *Studies in Second Language Acquisition*, 16: 205–50.

Carroll, D. W. 1999. *Psychology of Language* (3rd edn.). Pacific Grove, CA: Brooks/Cole Publishing.

Cassanelli, L., and F. S. Abdikadir. 2007. 'Somalia: Education in transition'. *Bildhaan: An International Journal of Somali Studies*, 7: 91–125.

Castro-Caldas, A., K. M. Petersson, A. Reis, S. Stone-Elander, and M. Ingvar. 1998. 'The illiterate brain: Learning to read and write during childhood influences the functional organization of the adult brain'. *Brain*, 121: 1053–63.

Chanoff, S. 2008. 'Africa's "forgotten" refugees'. *Boston Globe*. May 13. Retrieved on May 13, 2008, from http://www.boston.com/news/world/blog/2008/05/africas_forgott.html

Chernick, M. R. 2007. *Bootstrap Methods: A Guide for Practitioners and Researchers* (2nd edn.). New York: John Wiley and Sons.

Chun, A., R. R. Day, A. Chenoweth, and S. Luppescu. 1982. 'Errors, interaction, and correction: A study of native–nonnative conversations'. *TESOL Quarterly*, 16: 537–47.

Clahsen, H., J. M. Meisel, and M. Pienemann. 1983. *Deutsch als Zweitsprache. Der Spracherwerb ausländischer Arbeiter*. Tübingen: Narr.

Coady, J. A., and J. L. Evans. 2008. 'Uses and interpretations of non-word repetition tasks in children with and without specific language impairments (SLI)'. *International Journal of Language & Communication Disorders*, 43/1: 1–40.

Collier, V. 1989. 'How long? A synthesis of research on academic achievement in a second language'. *TESOL Quarterly*, 23/3: 509–31.

Cowan, N. 1995. *Attention and Memory*. Oxford: Oxford University Press.

Cummins, J. 1979. 'Linguistic interdependence and the educational development of bilingual children'. *Review of Educational Research*, 49: 222–51.

Cummins, J. 1981. *Bilingualism and Minority Children*. Ontario: Ontario Institute for Studies in Education.

Cummins, J. 1991. 'Conversational and academic language proficiency in bilingual contexts', in J. H. Hulstijn and J. F. Malter (eds.), *Reading in Two Languages: AILA Review*, 8: 75–89.

Current Population Reports. 2001. Washington, DC: US Census Bureau.

de Gelder, B., J. Vroomen, and P. Bertelson. 1993. 'The effects of alphabetic-reading competence on language representation in bilingual Chinese subjects'. *Psychological Research*, 55: 315–21.

DeKeyser, R., and A. Juffs. 2005. 'Cognitive considerations in L2 learning', in E. Hinkel (ed.), *Handbook of Research in Second Language Learning and Teaching*. Mahwah, NJ: Lawrence Erlbaum Associates.

Dellatolas, G., L. W. Braga, G. dN. Souza, G. N. Filho, E. Queiroz, and G. Deloche. 2003. 'Cognitive consequences of early phase of literacy'. *Journal of the International Neuropsychological Society*, 9: 771–82.

Dickie, M. 2005. 'K'Naan in his own words: The twice-nominated Toronto rapper talks to us about the state of his art'. *Toronto Sun*, December 2. Retrieved on May 6, 2008, from http://africatrip.tribe.net/thread/52df1d54-bc71-42e4-a292-44b5f22e1361

Dooling, D., and R. Lachman. 1971. 'Effects of comprehension on retention of prose'. *Journal of Experimental Psychology*, 88: 216–22.

Doughty, C. 2001. 'The cognitive underpinnings of focus on form', in P. Robinson (ed.), *Cognition and Second Language Instruction*. Cambridge: Cambridge University Press.

Doughty, C., and J. Williams. 1998a. 'Pedagogical choices in focus on form', in C. Doughty and J. Williams (eds.), *Focus on Form in Classroom Second Language Acquisition*. Cambridge: Cambridge University Press.

Doughty, C., and J. Williams (eds.). 1998b. *Focus on Form in Classroom Second Language Acquisition*. Cambridge: Cambridge University Press.

Duff, P. A. 2002. 'The discursive co-construction of knowledge, identity, and difference: An ethnography of communication in the high school mainstream'. *Applied Linguistics*, 23/3: 289–322.

Duff, P., and M. Early. 1996. 'Problematics of classroom research across sociopolitical contexts', in J. Schachter and S. Gass (eds.), *Second Language Classroom Research: Issues and Opportunities*. Hillsdale, NJ: Lawrence Erlbaum Associates.

Durgunoğlu, A. Y., and B. Öney. 2002. 'Phonological awareness in literacy acquisition: It's not only for children'. *Scientific Studies of Reading*, 6/3: 245–66.

Efron, B., and R. J. Tibshirani. 1993. *An Introduction to the Bootstrap*. Monographs on Statistics and Applied Probability, #57. New York: Chapman and Hall.

Egi, T. 2007. 'Interpreting recasts as linguistic evidence: The roles of linguistic target, length, and degree of change'. *Studies in Second Language Acquisition*, 29: 511–37.

Ehri, L. C. 1993. 'How English orthography influence phonological knowledge as children learn to read and spell', in R. J. Scholes (ed.), *Literacy and Language Analysis*. Hillsdale, NJ: Lawrence Erlbaum Associates.

Eisenstein, M., N. Bailey, and C. Madden. 1982. 'It takes two: Contrasting tasks and contrasting structures'. *TESOL Quarterly*, 16/3: 381–93.

Ellis, N. (ed.). 1994. *Implicit and Explicit Learning of Languages*. San Diego, CA: Academic Press.

Ellis, N. 1996. 'Sequencing in SLA: Phonological memory, chunking, and points of order'. *Studies in Second Language Acquisition*, 18: 91–126.

Ellis, R. 1993. 'The structural syllabus and second language acquisition'. *TESOL Quarterly*, 27: 91–113.

Ellis, R. 1994. 'A theory of instructed language acquisition', in N. Ellis (ed.), *Implicit and Explicit Learning of Languages*. San Diego, CA: Academic Press.

Ellis, R. 2002. 'Does form-focused instruction affect the acquisition of implicit knowledge?' *Studies in Second Language Acquisition*, 24/2: 223–36.

Ellis, R., and Y. Sheen. 2006. 'Reexamining the role of recasts in second language acquisition'. *Studies in Second Language Acquisition*, 28: 575–600.

Ellis, R., S. Loewen, and R. Erlam. 2006. 'Implicit and explicit corrective feedback and the acquisition of L2 grammar'. *Studies in Second Language Acquisition*, 28: 339–68.

Epstein, W. 1961. 'The influence of syntactical structure on learning'. *American Journal of Psychology*, 74: 80–5.

Ervin-Tripp, S. M. 1970. 'Structure and process in language acquisition', in J. E. Alatis (ed.), *Report of the Twenty-First Annual Round Table Meeting on Linguistics and Language Studies*. Washington, DC: Georgetown University Press.

Fangen, K. 2006. 'Humiliation experienced by Somali refugees in Norway'. *Journal of Refugee Studies*, 19: 69–93.

Faux, N. (ed.). 2007. *Low-Educated Second Language and Literacy Acquisition: Research, Policy and Practice. Proceedings of the Second Annual Forum*. Richmond, VA: Literacy Institute at Virginia Commonwealth University.

Fleischman, H. L., and P. Hopstick. 1993. *Descriptive Study of Services to Limited English Proficient Students*. Arlington, VA: Development Associates.

Forster, K. 1987. 'Binding, plausibility, and modularity', in J. L. Garfield (ed.), *Modularity in Knowledge Representation and Natural-Language Understanding*. Cambridge, MA: MIT Press.

Gass, S. M. 1985. 'Task variation and nonnative/nonnative negotiation of meaning', in S. M. Gass and C. G. Madden (eds.), *Input in Second Language Acquisition*. Boston: Heinle and Heinle Publishers.

Gass, S. M., and L. Selinker. 2008. *Second Language Acquisition: An Introductory Course*, 3rd edn. Mawah, NJ: Lawrence Erlbaum Associates.

Gathercole, S., and A. Baddeley. 1993. *Working Memory and Language*. Hillsdale, NJ: Lawrence Erlbaum Associates.

Gee, J. P. 1991. 'Socio-cultural approaches to literacy (literacies)'. *Annual Review of Applied Linguistics*, 12: 31–48.

Gee, J. P. 2001. 'Foreword', in T. M. Kalmar, *Illegal Alphabets: Latino Migrants Crossing the Linguistic Border*. Mahwah, NJ: Lawrence Erlbaum Associates.

Good, P. I. 2001. *Resampling Methods: A Practical Guide to Data Analysis*. Boston: Birkhauser.

Goody, J. 1987. *The Interface between the Written and the Oral*. Cambridge: Cambridge University Press.

Goody, J., and I. Watt. 1968. 'The consequences of literacy', in J. Goody (ed.), *Literacy in Traditional Societies*. New York: Cambridge University Press.

Gumperz, J. J. 1992. 'Contextualization and understanding', in A. Duranti and C. Goodwin (eds.), *Rethinking Context: Language as an Interactive Phenomenon*. Cambridge: Cambridge University Press.

Halliday, M. A. K. 1989. *Spoken and Written Language*. Oxford: Oxford University Press.

Hansen, K. 2005. 'Impact of Literacy Level and Task Type on Oral L2 Recall Accuracy.' MA Thesis, University of Minnesota.

Havelock, E. 1978. 'The alphabetization of Homer', in E. Havelock and J. P. Hershbell (eds.), *Communication Arts in the Ancient World*. New York: Hastings House.

Heath, S. B. 1983. *Ways with Words: Language, Life and Work in Communities and Classrooms*. Cambridge: Cambridge University Press.

Hill, J. 1970. 'Foreign accents, language acquisition and cerebral dominance revisited'. *Language Learning*, 20: 237–48.

Ibrahim, A. 1999. 'Becoming black: Rap and hip-hop, race, gender, identity, and the politics of ESL learning'. *TESOL Quarterly*, 33/3: 349–69.

Izumi, S., and M. Bigelow. 2000. 'Does output promote noticing and second language acquisition?' *TESOL Quarterly*, 34: 239–78.

Jamieson, A., A. Curry, and G. Martinez. 2001. 'School enrollment in the United States: Social and economic characteristics of students: October, 1999', in *Current Population Reports*. Washington: US Census Bureau.

Jefferies, E., M. A. Lambon Ralph, and A. Baddeley. 2004. 'Automatic and controlled processing in sentence recall: The role of long-term and working memory'. *Journal of Memory and Language*, 51: 623–43.

Kail, M. 2002. 'Sentence processing studies and linguistic literacy'. *Journal of Child Language*, 29: 463–66.

Karmiloff-Smith, A. 1986. 'Some fundamental aspects of language acquisition after five', in P. Fletcher and M. Garman (eds.), *Studies in Language Acquisition*, 2nd rev. edn. Cambridge: Cambridge University Press.

Koda, K. 1989. 'The effects of transferred vocabulary knowledge on the development of L2 reading proficiency'. *Foreign Language Annals*, 22: 529–40.

Koda, K. 2005. *Insights into Second Language Reading*. Cambridge: Cambridge University Press.

Kolinsky, R., L. Cary, and J. Morais. 1987. 'Awareness of words as phonological entities: The role of literacy'. *Applied Psycholinguistics*, 8: 223–32.

Kosmidis, M. H., K. Tsapkini, V. Folia, C. Vlahou, and G. Kiosseoglou. 2004. 'Semantic and phonological processing in illiteracy'. *Journal of the Neuropsychological Society*, 10: 818–27.

Kowal, M., and M. Swain. 1997. 'From semantic to syntactic processing: How can we promote it in the immersion classroom?', in R. K. Johnson and M. Swain (eds.), *Immersion Education: International Perspectives*. New York: Cambridge University Press.

Krashen, S. D. 1981. *Second Language Acquisition and Second Language Learning*. London: Pergamon Press.

Krashen, S. D. 1982. *Principles and Practice in Second Language Acquisition*. Englewood Cliffs, NJ: Prentice-Hall International.

Krashen, S. D. 1985. *The Input Hypothesis: Issues and Implications*. New York: Longman.

Krashen, S. D. 1994. 'The input hypothesis and its rivals', in N. Ellis (ed.), *Implicit and Explicit Learning of Languages*. San Diego, CA: Academic Press.

Kusow, A. M. 2006. 'Migration and racial formations among Somali immigrants in North America'. *Journal of Ethnic and Migration Studies*, 32/3: 533–51.

Lantolf, J. P. 2000a. 'Introducing sociocultural theory', in J. P. Lantolf (ed.), *Sociocultural Theory and Second Language Learning*. Oxford: Oxford University Press.

Lantolf, J. P. (ed.). 2000b. *Sociocultural Theory and Second Language Learning*. Oxford: Oxford University Press.

Lantolf, J. P., and M. K. Ahmed. 1989. 'Psycholinguistic perspectives on interlanguage variation: A Vygotskyan analysis', in S. Gass, C. Madden, D. R. Preston, and L. Selinker (eds.). *Variation in Second Language Acquisition: Psycholinguistic Issues*. Philadelphia, PA: Multilingual Matters.

Lee, L. L. 1970. 'A screening test for syntax development'. *Journal of Speech and Hearing Disorders*, 35/2: 102–12.

Levelt, W. 1992. 'Accessing words in speech productions: Stages, processes, and presentations'. *Cognition*, 42: 1–22.

Liberman, A. M., F. S. Cooper, D. P. Shankweiler, and M. Studdert-Kennedy. 1967. 'Perception of speech code'. *Psychological Review*, 74: 431–61.

Loewen, S., and J. Philp. 2006. 'Recasts in the adult English L2 classroom: Characteristics, explicitness and effectiveness'. *Modern Language Journal*, 90: 536–56.

Long, M. H. 1980. 'Input, Interaction and Second language Acquisition'. Ph.D. Dissertation, UCLA, Los Angeles.

Long, M. H. 1990. 'The least a second language acquisition theory needs to explain'. *TESOL Quarterly*, 24: 649–66.

Long, M. H. 1991. 'Focus of form: A design feature in language teaching methodology', in K. de Bot, R. B. Ginsberg, and C. Kramsch (eds.), *Foreign Language Research in Cross-Cultural Perspectives*. Amsterdam: John Benjamins.

Long, M. H. 1998. 'SLA: Breaking the Siege'. University of Hawaii Working Papers in ESL 17: 79–129.

Long, M. H., and P. Robinson. 1998. 'Focus on form: Theory, research and practice', in C. Doughty and J. Williams (eds.), *Focus on Form in Classroom Second Language Acquisition*. Cambridge: Cambridge University Press.

Long, M. H., S. Inagaki, and L. Ortega. 1998. 'The role of implicit negative feedback in SLA: Models and recasts in Japanese and Spanish'. *Modern Language Journal*, 82: 357–71.

Loureiro, C. dS., L. W. Braga, G. dN. Souza, G. N. Filho, E. Queiroz, and G. Dellatolas. 2004. 'Degree of illiteracy and phonological and metaphonological skills in unschooled adults'. *Brain and Language*, 89: 499–502.

Luria, A. R. 1976. *Cognitive Development: Its Cultural and Social Foundations*. Cambridge, MA: Harvard University Press.

Lust, B., Y. Chien, and S. Flynn. 1987. 'What children know: Methods for the study of first language acquisition', in B. Lust (ed.), *Studies in the Acquisition of Anaphora*, vol. II. Dordrecht: D. Reidel Publishing Company.

Lyster, R. 1998a. 'Form in immersion classroom discourse: In or out of focus?' *Canadian Journal of Applied Linguistics*, 1: 53–82.

Lyster, R. 1998b. 'Recasts, repetition and ambiguity in L2 classroom discourse'. *Studies in Second Language Acquisition*, 20: 51–80.

Lyster, R. 1998c. 'Negotiation of form, recasts, and explicit correction in relation to error types and learner repair in immersion classrooms'. *Language Learning*, 48: 183–218.

Lyster, R. 2004. 'Differential effects of prompts and recasts in form-focused instruction'. *Studies in Second Language Acquisition*, 26: 399–432.

Lyster, R. and L. Ranta. 1997. 'Corrective feedback and learner uptake: Negotiation of form in communicative classrooms'. *Studies in Second Language Acquisition*, 19: 37–66.

McDonough, K. and A. Mackey. 2006. 'Responses to recasts: Repetitions, primed production, and linguistic development'. *Language Learning*, 56: 693–720.

McHugh, M., J. Gelatt, and M. Fix. 2007. 'Adult English language instruction in the United States: Determining need and investing wisely'. Washington, DC: Migration Policy Institute.

Mackey, A. 1999. 'Input, interaction, and second language development: An empirical study of question formation in ESL'. *Studies in Second Language Acquisition*, 21: 557–87.

Mackey, A., S. Gass, and K. McDonough. 2000. 'How do learners perceive interactional feedback?' *Studies in Second Language Acquisition*, 22: 471–98.

Marks, L. E., and G. Miller. 1964. 'The role of semantic and syntactic constraints in the memorization of English sentences'. *Journal of Verbal Learning and Verbal Behavior*, 3: 1–5.

Mathews, R. C. 1991. 'The forgetting algorithm: How fragmentary knowledge of exemplars can yield abstract knowledge'. *Journal of Experimental Psychology: General*, 120: 117–19.

Meisel, J. M., H. Clahsen, and M. Pienemann. 1981. 'On determining developmental stages in natural second language acquisition'. *Studies in Second Language Acquisition*, 3: 109–35.

Miller, G. 1956. 'The magical number seven, plus or minus two: Some limits on our capacity for processing information'. *Psychological Review* 63: 81–97.

Miller, G., and J. A. Selfridge. 1950. 'Verbal context and the recall of meaningful material'. *American Journal of Psychology*, 63: 176–85.

Miller, J. 2002. 'Questions about constructions'. *Journal of Child Language*, 29: 470–4.

Morais, J., L. Cary, J. Alegría, and P. Bertelson. 1979. 'Does awareness of speech as a sequence of phones arise spontaneously?' *Cognition*, 7: 323–31.

Morais, J., P. Bertelson, L. Cary, and J. Alegría. 1986. 'Literacy training and speech segmentation'. *Cognition*, 24: 45–64.

Munnich, E., S. Flynn, and G. Martohardjono. 1994. 'Elicited imitation and grammaticality judgment tasks: What they measure and how they relate to each other', in E. Tarone, S. M. Gass, and A. D. Cohen (eds.), *Research Methodology in Second-Language Acquisition*. Hillsdale, NJ: Lawrence Erlbaum Associates.

Naiman, N. 1974. 'The use of elicited imitation in second language acquisition'. *Working Papers on Bilingualism*, 2: 2–37.

Natalicio, D. 1979. 'Repetition and dictation as language testing techniques'. *Modern Language Journal*, 64: 165–76.

Native Language Literacy Screening Device. n.d. Glenmont, NY: Hudson River Center for Program Development (102 Mosher Road, Glenmont, NY 12077–4202).

Nelson, K. E. 1987. 'Some observations from the perspective of the rare event cognitive comparison theory of language acquisition', in K. E. Nelson and A. V. Kleek (eds.), *Children's Language*. Hillsdale, NJ: Lawrence Erlbaum Associates.

Norris, J., and L. Ortega. 2000. 'Effectiveness of L2 instruction: A research synthesis and quantitative meta-analysis'. *Language Learning*, 50/3: 417–528.

Norris, J., and L. Ortega. 2001. 'Does type of instruction make a difference? Substantive findings from a meta-analytic review'. *Language Learning*, 51 (Supplement 1): 157–213.

Ohta, A. S. 2001. *Second Language Acquisition Processes in the Classroom: Learning Japanese*. Mahwah, NJ: Lawrence Erlbaum Associates.

Olson, D. 1994. *The World on Paper*. Cambridge: Cambridge University Press.

Olson, D. 2002. 'What writing does to the mind', in E. Amsel and J. Byrnes (eds.), *Language, Literacy, and Cognitive Development: The Development and Consequences of Symbolic Communication*. Mahwah, NJ: Lawrence Erlbaum Associates.

Olson, D., and N. Torrance (eds.). 1991. *Literacy and Orality*. Cambridge: Cambridge University Press.

Ong, W. J. 1982. *Orality and Literacy: The Technologizing of the Word*. London: Methuen.

Paradis, M. 1994. 'Neurolinguistic aspects of implicit and explicit memory: Implications for bilingualism and SLA', in N. Ellis (ed.), *Implicit and Explicit Learning of Languages*. San Diego, CA: Academic Press.

Perdue, C. 1993. *Adult Language Acquisition: Cross-Linguistic Perspectives*. Cambridge: Cambridge University Press.

Philp, J. 1999. 'Interaction, noticing and second language acquisition: An examination of learners' noticing of recasts in task-based interaction'. Unpublished doctoral dissertation, University of Tasmania, Australia.

Philp, J. 2003. 'Constraints on "noticing the gap": Nonnative speakers' noticing of recasts in NS–NNS interaction'. *Studies in Second Language Acquisition*, 25: 99–126.

Piaget, J. 1929. *The Child's Conception of the World*. New York: Harcourt Brace.

Pica, T. 1983. 'Adult acquisition of English as a second language under different conditions of exposure'. *Language Learning*, 33:465–97.

Pienemann, M. 2005. 'An introduction to processability theory', in M. Pienemann (ed.), *Cross-Linguistic Aspects of Processability Theory*. Amsterdam: John Benjamins Publishing Co.

Pienemann, M., and M. Johnston. 1987. 'Factors influencing the development of language proficiency', in D. Nunan (ed.), *Applying Second Language Acquisition Research*. Adelaide, Australia: National Curriculum Resource Centre.

Pienemann, M., M. Johnston, and G. Brindley. 1988. 'Constructing an acquisition-based procedure for second language assessment'. *Studies in Second Language Acquisition*, 10: 217–43.

Preston, D. 2000. 'Three kinds of sociolinguistics and SLA: A psycholinguistic perspective', in F. M. B. Swierzbin, M. Anderson, C. Klee, and E. Tarone (eds.), *Social and Cognitive Factors in Second Language Acquisition: Selected Proceedings of the 1999 Second Language Research Forum*. Somerville, MA: Cascadilla.

Preston, D. 2002. 'A variationist perspective on SLA: Psycholinguistic concerns', in R. Kaplan (ed.), *Oxford Handbook of Applied Linguistics*. Oxford: Oxford University Press.

Preston, D. and Fasold, R. 2007. 'The psycholinguistic unity of inherent variability: Old Occam whips out his razor', in R. Bayley and C. Lucas (eds.), *Sociolinguistic Variation: Theory, Methods, and Applications*. Cambridge: Cambridge University Press, 45–69.

Randall, M. 2007. *Memory, Psychology and Second Language Learning*. Amsterdam: John Benjamins.

Ravid, D., and L. Tolchinsky. 2002. 'Developing linguistic literacy: A comprehensive model'. *Journal of Child Language*, 29: 417–47.

Read, C., Y. Zhang, H. Nie, and B. Ding. 1986. 'The ability to manipulate speech sounds depends on knowing alphabetic spelling'. *Cognition*, 24: 31–44.

Reber, A. S. 1993. *Implicit Learning and Tacit Knowledge*. New York and Oxford: Oxford University Press.

Reis, A., and A. Castro-Caldas. 1997. 'Illiteracy: A cause for biased cognitive development'. *Journal of the International Neuropsychological Society*, 3: 444–50.

Robson, B. 1982. 'Hmong literacy, formal education, and their effects on performance in an ESL class', in B. Downing and D. Olney (eds.), *The Hmong in the West: Observations and Reports*. Minneapolis: CURA, University of Minnesota, 201–25.

Romaine, S. 1984. *The Language of Children and Adolescents: The Acquisition of Communicative Competence*. Oxford: Blackwell.

Rounds, P. 1996. 'The classroom-based researcher as fieldworker', in J. Schachter and S. Gass (eds.), *Second Language Classroom Research*. Mahwah, NJ: Lawrence Erlbaum Associates.

Sanders, E. 2007. 'Unsung hero shines light of learning in Somalia'. *Los Angeles Times*. November 17. Retrieved on March 20, 2008, from http://www.startribune.com/world/11829526.html

Saxton, M. 1997. 'The contrast theory of negative input'. *Journal of Child Language*, 24: 139–61.

Schmidt, R. W. 1990. 'The role of consciousness in second language learning'. *Applied Linguistics*, 11: 129–58.

Schmidt, R. W. 1993. 'Awareness and second language acquisition'. *Annual Review of Applied Linguistics*, 13: 206–26.

Schmidt, R. W. 1994a. 'Deconstructing consciousness in search of useful definitions for applied linguistics'. *AILA Review: Consciousness and Second Language Learning: Conceptual, Methodological and Practical Issues in Language Learning and Teaching*, 11: 11–26.

Schmidt, R. W. 1994b. 'Implicit learning and the cognitive unconscious: Of artificial grammars and SLA', in N. Ellis (ed.), *Implicit and Explicit Learning of Languages*. San Diego, CA: Academic Press.

Schmidt, R. W. 1995a. 'Consciousness and foreign language learning: A tutorial on the role of attention and awareness in learning', in R. W. Schmidt (ed.), *Attention and Awareness in Foreign Language Learning (Vol. Technical Report #9)*. Honolulu: University of Hawai'i Press.

Schmidt, R. W. (ed.). 1995b. *Attention and Awareness in Foreign Language Learning (Vol. Technical Report #9)*. Honolulu: University of Hawai'i Press.

Schmidt, R. W. 2001. 'Attention', in P. Robinson (ed.), *Cognition and Second Language Instruction*. Cambridge: Cambridge University Press.

Scholes, R. J. 1998. 'The case against phonemic awareness'. *Journal of Research in Reading*, 21: 177–88.

Scribner, S., and M. Cole. 1981. *The Psychology of Literacy*. Cambridge, MA: Harvard University Press.

Sharwood Smith, M. 1981. 'Consciousness raising and the second language learner'. *Applied Linguistics*, 2: 159–68.

Sharwood Smith, M. 1991. 'Speaking to many minds: On the relevance of different types of language information for the L2 learner'. *Second Language Research*, 7: 118–32.

Sharwood Smith, M. 1993. 'Input enhancement in instructed SLA: Theoretical bases'. *Studies in Second Language Acquisition*, 15: 165–79.

Short, D., and S. Fitzsimmons. 2007. *Double the Work: Challenges and Solutions to Acquiring Language and Academic Literacy for Adolescent English Language Learners*. New York: Carnegie Corporation of New York.

Snowling, M. J. 1998. 'Reading development and its difficulties'. *Educational and Child Psychology*, 15: 44–58.

Sokolov, J. L., and C. Snow. 1994. 'The changing role of negative evidence in theories of language development', in C. Gallaway and B. J. Richards (eds.), *Input and Interaction in Language Acquisition*. Cambridge: Cambridge University Press.

Soon, C. S., M. Brass, H. J. Heinze, and J. D. Haynes. 2008. 'Unconscious determinants of free decisions in the human brain'. *Nature Neuroscience*, 11: 543–5.

Speaking Proficiency English Assessment Kit (SPEAK). 1982. Educational Testing Service. Princeton, NY, 08541.

Stadler, M. A., and P. A. Frensch. 1998. 'Preface', in M. A. Stadler and P. A. Frensch (eds.), *Handbook of Implicit Learning*. Thousand Oaks, CA: Sage Publications.

Street, B. V. 1995. *Social Literacies: Critical Approaches to Literacy in Development, Ethnography, and Education*. London: Longman.

Street, B. V. 2003. 'What's "new" in new literacy studies? Critical approaches to literacy in theory and practice'. *Current Issues in Comparative Education*, 5/2: 77–91.

Swain, M. 1995. 'Three functions of output in second language learning', in G. Cook and
  B. Seidlhofer (eds.), *Principle and Practice in Applied Linguistics: Studies in Honour
  of H. G. Widdowson*. Oxford: Oxford University Press.

Swain, M. 2000. 'The output hypothesis and beyond: Mediating acquisition through
  collaborative dialogue', in J. P. Lantolf (ed.), *Sociocultural Theory and Second Language
  Learning*. Oxford: Oxford University Press.

Swain, M., and S. Lapkin. 1995. 'Problems in output and the cognitive processes they generate:
  A step towards second language learning'. *Applied Linguistics*, 16: 371–91.

Swain, M., G. Dumas, and N. Naiman. 1974. 'Alternatives to spontaneous speech: Elicited
  translation and imitation as indicators of second language competence'. *Working Papers on
  Bilingualism*, 3: 68–79.

Swierzbin, B. 2004. 'The Role of Cognitive Status in Second Language Acquisition of
  English Noun Phrase Referring Expressions'. Ph.D. Dissertation, Linguistics, University of
  Minnesota, Minneapolis.

Swierzbin, B., F. Morris, M. Anderson, C. Klee, and E. Tarone (eds.). 2000. *Social and
  Cognitive Factors in SLA: Proceedings of the 1999 Second Language Research Forum*.
  Somerville, MA: Cascadilla.

Tarone, E. 1979. 'Interlanguage as chameleon'. *Language Learning*, 29: 181–91.

Tarone, E. 1980. 'Communication strategies, foreigner talk and repair in interlanguage'.
  Language Learning, 30: 417–32.

Tarone, E. 1985. 'Variability in interlanguage use: A study of style-shifting in morphology and
  syntax'. *Language Learning*, 35: 373–403.

Tarone, E. 2000a. 'Getting serious about language play: Language play, interlanguage
  variation and second language acquisition', in B. Swierzbin, F. Morris, M. Anderson,
  C. Klee, and E. Tarone (eds.), *Social and Cognitive Factors in SLA: Proceedings of the 1999
  Second Language Research Forum*. Somerville, MA: Cascadilla.

Tarone, E. 2000b. 'Still wrestling with "context" in interlanguage theory'. *Annual Review of
  Applied Linguistics*, 20: 182–98.

Tarone, E. 2007. 'Sociolinguistic approaches to second language acquisition research,
  1997–2007'. *Modern Language Journal, Focus Issue: Second Language Acquisition
  Reconceptualized: The Impact of Firth and Wagner (1997)*, 91: 837–48.

Tarone, E. forthcoming. 'Social context and cognition in SLA: A variationist perspective', in
  R. Batstone (ed.), *Sociocognitive Perspectives on Language Use and Language Learning*.
  Oxford: Oxford University Press.

Tarone, E., and M. Bigelow. 2005. 'Impact of literacy on oral language processing:
  Implications for SLA research'. *Annual Review of Applied Linguistics*, 25: 77–97.

Tarone, E., and M. Bigelow. 2007. 'Alphabetic print literacy and processing of oral corrective
  feedback in L2 interaction', in A. Mackey (ed.), *Conversational Interaction in Second
  Language Acquisition: A Series of Empirical Studies*. Oxford: Oxford University Press.

Tarone, E., M. Bigelow, and K. Hansen. 2007. 'The impact of alphabetic print literacy level
  on oral second language acquisition' in N. Faux (ed.), *Low-Educated Second Language
  and Literacy Acquisition: Research, Policy and Practice. Proceedings of the Second Annual
  Forum*. Richmond, VA: Literacy Institute at Virginia Commonwealth University.

Tarone, E., S. M. Gass, and A. D. Cohen (eds.). 1994. *Research Methodology in Second-
  language Acquisition*. Hillsdale, NJ: Lawrence Erlbaum Associates.

Tarone, E., B. Swierzbin, and M. Bigelow. 2006. 'The impact of literacy level on features of
  interlanguage in oral narratives'. *Rivista di Psicolinguistica Applicata*, 6/3: 65–77. (Thomas
  Baldwin and Larry Selinker, eds.) *Special Issue on 'Interlanguage: Current Thought and
  Practices*.

Thompkins, A. C., and K. S. Binder. 2003. 'A comparison of the factors affecting reading
  performance of functionally illiterate adults and children matched by reading level'. *Reading
  Research Quarterly*, 38: 236–58.

Tomlin, R. S., and V. Villa. 1994. 'Attention in cognitive science and second language
  acquisition'. *Studies in Second Language Acquisition*, 16: 183–203.

UNICEF. n.d. *Despite all Odds*. Retrieved on May 14, 2008, from www.unicef.org/somalia/SOM_NewDawndoc.pdf

Van de Craats, I., J. Kurvers, and M. Young-Scholten (eds.). 2006. *Low-Educated Second Language and Literacy Acquisition: Research, Policy and Practice*. Occasional Series 6. Utrecht: LOT.

Verhoeven, L. 1994. 'Transfer in bilingual development: The linguistic interdependence hypothesis revisited'. *Language Learning*, 44: 381–415.

Verhoeven, L. 2002. 'Sociocultural and cognitive constraints on literacy development'. *Journal of Child Language*, 29: 484–8.

Vinther, T. 2002. 'Elicited imitation: A brief overview'. *International Journal of Applied Linguistics*, 12/1: 54–73.

Vygotsky, L. S. 1962. *Thought and Language*. Cambridge, MA: MIT Press.

Vygotsky, L. S. 1978. *Mind in Society: The Development of Higher Psychological Processes*, ed. M. Cole, V. John-Steiner, S. Scribner, and E. Souberman. Cambridge, MA: Harvard University Press.

Wang, M., K. Koda, and C. A. Perfetti. 2003. 'Alphabetic and nonalphabetic L1 effects in English word identification: A comparison of Korean and Chinese English L2 learners'. *Cognition*, 87: 129–49.

Warsame, A. A. 2001. 'How a strong government backed an African language: The lessons of Somalia'. *International Review of Education*, 47/3–4: 341–60.

Whorf, B. L. 1956. 'Science and linguistics', in *Selected Writings of Benjamin Lee Whorf*. Cambridge, MA: MIT Press.

Wiley, T. G. 2005. 'Second language literacy and biliteracy', in E. Hinkel (ed.), *Handbook of Research in Second Language Teaching and Learning*. Hillsdale, NJ: Lawrence Erlbaum Associates.

Yang, K. K. 2008. *The Late Homecomer: A Hmong Family Memoir*. Minneapolis: Coffee House Press.

Yule, G. 1997. *Referential Communication Tasks*. Cambridge: Cambridge University Press.

Zobl, H. 1995. 'Converging evidence for the "acquisition-learning" distinction'. *Applied Linguistics*, 16: 35–56.

Author Index

See the subject index for research participants, names of research projects and organizations. References to tables and notes are entered as, for example, 104t, 5n.

Subject Index

References to chapter notes are entered as, for example, 5n; references to tables and figures are indicated by 't' and 'f' respectively, for example 22t, 49f. Tables and figures are indexed separately only if they contain information that is found nowhere else on that page.